MANAGERS WITH GOD

To Esther & Leon - dear friends & colleagues!

Dan K

MANAGERS WITH GOD

CONTINUING THE WORK CHRIST BEGAN

DANIEL KAUFFMAN

HERALD PRESS
Scottdale, Pennsylvania
Waterloo, Ontario

Library of Congress Cataloging-in-Publication Data

Kauffman, Daniel, 1922-
    Managers with God : continuing the work Christ began /
        Daniel Kauffman. p. cm.
    Includes bibliographical references.
    ISBN 0-8361-3518-0 (alk. paper) :
    1. Stewardship, Christian. 2. Christian giving. 3. Church
        finance. 4. Church growth. I. Title.
    BV772.K29 1990
    254.8—dc20   89-77249
                                                                CIP

The paper used in this publication meets the minimum
requirements of American National Standard for Information
Sciences—Permanence of Paper for Printed Library Materials,
ANSI Z39.48-1984.

MANAGERS WITH GOD
Copyright © 1990 by Herald Press, Scottdale, Pa. 15683
        Published simultaneously in Canada by Herald Press,
        Waterloo, Ont. N2L 6H7. All rights reserved except that
        charts and forms may be reproduced for use in
        congregations.
Library of Congress Catalog Card Number: 89-77249
International Standard Book Number: 0-8361-3518-0
Printed in the United States of America
Cover and book design by Gwen M. Stamm

97 96 95 94 93 92 91 90 10 9 8 7 6 5 4 3 2 1

To my mother,
Mabel E. Kauffman,
and to the memory of my father,
James A. Kauffman (deceased 1933),
who discovered early in their lives
the importance of Christian belief,
faith, and dedication.

As you go, preach this message:
"The kingdom of heaven is near."

Heal the sick,
Raise the dead,
Cleanse those who have leprosy,
Drive out demons.

Freely you have received,
Freely give.

(Matthew 10:7-8)

He has committed to us
the message of reconciliation.
We are therefore Christ's ambassadors,
as though God is making his appeal through us.

(2 Corinthians 5:19-20)

Contents

Foreword

CHRISTIAN stewardship is frequently misunderstood. So often it is limited to giving or tithing or annual fund drives. In the name of stewardship all sorts of schemes are devised to relieve people of their worldly possessions.

Dan Kauffman brings fresh clarity to Christian stewardship. He helps us understand the Scriptures. He elevates stewardship to the place it deserves in our congregaions. He breathes new dignity and relevance into divine truth.

Most Christians believe in stewardship. They listen to countless sermons. It is taught in Sunday school classes. There is a deluge of literature. But how does stewardship become practical in all of life, in our own everyday behavior? How does it impact all we are and all we have?

Here is where Dan Kauffman is so helpful. Not only does he open up the profound meaning and sweeping implications of stewardship, but he quickly proceeds

to an arena where we are in most need of help: the practical applications, the how-to suggestions, the specific methods.

When it comes to personal expressions of Christian stewardship, Dan is more than just talk. He models stewardship in his own life. He lives it. He demonstrates it. He's a visual aid. His book grows out of a whole lifetime of living and teaching faithful stewardship.

Because of Dan's many years of experience in helping congregations and church institutions, specific parts of his book deserve special attention: firstfruits and Jubilee giving; money and economic issues; creative vehicles for charitable giving; teaching stewardship in congregations; financing the church.

All of us ought to listen carefully to Dan Kauffman. He shares sound counsel and much wisdom. His book should help further the stewardship movement in our personal, congregational, and institutional lives.

I commend this book to pastors, teachers, congregational leaders, and many others throughout the church. It is my hope and prayer that Dan's book will help nudge many of us toward the stewardship revival we so much need.

> *John H. Rudy*
> *Stewardship Minister/Financial Counselor*
> *Mennonite Foundation*
> *Lancaster, Pennsylvania*

Author's Preface

A NUMBER of years ago a friend and I were discussing life choices. He said, "You know, the massive gates of circumstance turn upon the smallest hinge."

"Wow!" I responded. "Say that again!" I knew the statement needed more reflection.

What small hinges or influences in our lives turn to open up career and service opportunities, lifestyles, relationships, and new geographic places for service? For many of us, these hinges are so small we scarcely notice them. Yet they are powerful. Our childhood dreams; our role models and heroes; the positive and negative experiences in our homes, churches, or schools—all influence our choices. Current events, neighbors, friends, a supportive or negative glance or comment from a person we respect—any of these can have a profound impact on us.

I have had a lifelong interest in business and industry. In my youth I dreamed of being a corporate executive. Because of the draft and World War II, a small hinge began to turn a series of gates which opened new opportunities I never would have imagined at age twenty-three.

A person does not receive a call to devote a lifetime to Christian stewardship without events creating a special climate for change. That call to give my life to helping persons become better stewards was certainly circumstantial. In stewardship work I have experienced successes and failures. Both have enriched my life. They have helped me to develop an administrative style and teaching approach that have been useful in denominational and congregational administration as well as Christian college development.

Recently many persons have asked me to share my approaches and beliefs in a broader way, through a book or a "how to" manual. I am not a writer or a teacher. And I'm certainly not a theologian. I'm a practitioner who believes that God uses our experiences in life to guide us in a certain way, providing we are open to his will and direction.

Persons reading the stewardship studies and approaches in Chapters 2 through 11 will not understand the approach unless they know something of my past. Often I have read a book and wondered why the author said it that way. I'm sure that writer's background and experience held the answer.

For this reason I will share with you a part of my own faith story in Chapter 1. You will discover some very small hinges turning large and massive gates of opportunity in my life. The issues and experiences I have gone through confirm what I believe and teach. I hope my life also demonstrates it.

I wrote Chapters 2 through 11 for all Christian traditions. I have worked in the Christian Disciples of Christ, Church of the Brethren, United Church of Christ, Episcopal, Mennonite, Methodist, and Presbyterian denominations. Christian stewardship is not sectarian. Stewardship is the call for us to be faithful to the high calling of Jesus Christ. God bless us all toward this end!

I acknowledge my indebtedness to various teachers and friends whose sayings I have remembered and incorporated in my presentations.

I would like to express my sincere gratitude to Milo Kauffman, my pastor while I was growing up as a teenager. His kind and loving ways demonstrated that Christianity is to be lived between the Sundays. Later he became my mentor as I studied and developed my own biblical view of Christian stewardship.

My wife, Edith, gave me enthusiastic support through those long years (1946 to 1961) in the search for a better way to finance the church. She was a strong encouragement during the recent years (1961 to 1987) in our growing understanding that we are stewards of the gospel. (Edith passed away April 2, 1988.)

Finally, I want to thank the following friends for reading and evaluating my manuscript: Ray and Lillian Bair, J. Lawrence Burkholder, Rachel Fisher, Marlin Jeschke, Robert Johnson, John Rudy, Gary Shetler, James Waltner, Greg Weaver, and Gordon Zook. I also thank Gladie Burkhart, Melba Numemaker and Cynthia Pergrem for typing the manuscript.

Daniel Kauffman
Goshen, Indiana
January 1989

1

Gates, Circumstances, and Hinges

A Personal Story

AS A SMALL boy on a Kansas farm, I dreamed of someday being a businessman. And not just an ordinary businessman. I dreamed of being an executive with Ford Motor Company or John Deere. Why Ford or Deere? I'm not sure. Ten-year-old boys are not always realistic. I suspect it was because I admired the John Deere equipment most farmers had and the Ford cars and pickups nearly everyone drove in our small farming community.

In high school I took all the courses offered in business, bookkeeping, and salesmanship. In college I majored in economics. I still planned to enter business, but the Ford and Deere dreams faded. They had served their purpose by keeping my mind on business as I planned for the future.

World War II was in progress at that time. I was drafted in 1943 and assigned to the Nursing School of Alexian Brothers Hospital in Chicago where I later graduated as a nurse. Because I was short 15 credit hours of completing college, I also enrolled in the night school of Northwestern University School of Business. I completed my degree in economics in the fall of 1945.

How does a young man with a nursing and economics background enter business? Some local Chicago counselors suggested I enroll at Northwestern University for a master's degree in hospital administration. That caught my fancy, so with the help of scholarships, I enrolled.

My future was certain, I thought. There would be ample opportunities for employment in this *big* field. A hospital administrator with a nursing background should be in demand, I reasoned. Further, I was staying in my field of business!

However, my dream was short-lived. One day I received a letter from a Goshen College faculty member I admired. He strongly encouraged me to accept the business manager's position at Hesston College, in central Kansas. I had turned down the Hesston offer several times earlier, telling the president I was too young—twenty-three at the time. This time my wife and I reconsidered.

Suddenly we were on our way to Hesston College. We committed ourselves for only one year. But that year turned into a fifteen-year tenure. That letter was a small hinge which swung a massive gate!

The Search for a New Way

Milo Kauffman was president of Hesston College. We worked together well. He was an experienced church leader and served as a role model for me in those early years.

My job was difficult and demanding. Our board and administration were committed to quality Christian education, but it was hard to attract qualified faculty because of Hesston's low pay scale. Every hour of every day we saw opportunities to improve the education for our students, but there were not enough dollars to develop a better college. I worked long hours trying to find ways for new sources of income, ways to increase the student body, ways to make our operation more efficient.

I spent many weeks on the road each year, going door-to-door asking for money and new students. Our territory was the entire western half of the United States and the four western provinces of Canada.

Our fund-raising approach was simple. I would speak in a Mennonite Church on Sunday morning or evening or weekday evening to tell Hesston's story. The following day(s) I visited every congregational household to pick up contributions and encourage sons and daughters to enroll. I visited nearly every Mennonite home west of the Mississippi River.

After each trip I walked into President Kauffman's office to report on my efforts. I always closed these sessions by saying, "Milo, there has to be a better way to finance this college!" He would answer, "Yes, Dan. Find a better way!"

The answer was not forthcoming. My wife and I often wept as we tried to find the solution. We would welcome any plan that would end my annual door-to-door "tin-cupping."

During the 1940s and '50s, the Mennonite Church's financial plan was not coordinated. Each congregation approved a Sunday offering schedule a year in advance. For example, a congregation might approve something like this:

	Purpose of Offering
1st Sunday of the month	pastoral support
2nd Sunday	local operating expenses
3rd Sunday	world missions
4th Sunday	overseas relief
5th Sunday	district conference work

In the 1920s many congregations needed only one offering each month. As the church's ministry expanded, it was easy to add offerings on the other three Sundays to meet additional needs. Eventually each Sunday offering went to a cause. Sometimes a congregation collected even second and third offerings on a given Sunday. I was in one congregation where they took five offerings one Sunday morning! This was their way to respond to the newly emerging programs in church camping, youth work, Mennonite Central Committee activities, world peace issues, building funds, and more. But they never included higher education!

Why our congregations were afraid of a unified budget that would include our colleges was a mystery to me. In the Mennonite Church a unified budget was considered "worldly." It was the way churches of the world did it, I was told so often. No one was about to add our church colleges to the schedule of church offerings, so my annual house-to-house solicitation for higher education continued—as did my frustration.

A Break on the Horizon

During the 1956–1957 school year I received a sabbatical leave for additional graduate study. I chose to work on my master's degree in Higher Educational Administration at Columbia University, New York City.

This was a welcome release from the ever-present financial pressures of the college. Of course, New York was a different world from the plains of Kansas, so we went with some anxiety.

We lived in university-owned housing just off North Broadway in upper Manhattan. The Columbia University campus was west of us. Union Theological Seminary was one block north and Riverside Church one-and-a-half blocks north.

Back in Kansas we had decided to be church tramps during our year in New York. That is, we were going to attend many churches to see how the New Yorkers did it. On our first Sunday we thought, "Why not go to the closest church—Riverside?" It had an impressive tower, and since it was known as the Harry Emerson Fosdick church, we knew it would be a different experience for us. What we did not know was *how* different the experience would be. We were warmly welcomed by the greeter at the door. The singing, the prayers, the choir, and the sermon by Pastor Robert McCracken were exactly what this nervous little family from Kansas needed. In fact, we never did get to another church's services. We were hesitant to leave Riverside, fearing another church experience would not be as meaningful for us.

During the week, on my way to the Columbia Library for study each morning, I would stop at the Union Seminary chapel for a twenty-minute chapel service. I would listen to such persons as Paul Tillich, Lewis Sherrill, and Reinhold Niebuhr. Tillich often spoke on the theological meaning of a person's gifts, including money and wealth. It was new to me to think that wealth had theological significance.

In fact, much was new to me that year. I was eager to return to Hesston to put to work my new under-

standings of educational administration, policy formation, financial management, personnel administration,
and board and faculty relationships.

But there was still a void in my learning. I still
needed help on how to finance a church college like
Hesston. Our approach to funding was different from
the typical American college and I had found no help
at Columbia for our peculiar problem.

In desperation I contacted the Lutheran Church of
America headquarters in downtown Manhattan. They
had many colleges, some of which were not too different from Hesston. I arranged a meeting for the following week with Dr. Henry Endress, an educator and the
director of the Lutheran Laity Movement.

Dr. Endress was an idea person. He was exactly
what I'd hoped for. He listened to my problem, then
began to suggest some solutions. "Tie your college to
a cause bigger than you are," he said. "Connect it to
the destiny of the church." Church agencies usually
talk about the big financial problems they have balanc-
ing their budgets, he told me. They may even say, "If
you don't give more, we will have to retrench."

"This approach is not motivating," Dr. Endress told
me. "People don't give to needs or threats as much as
they give to dreams, to visions of what a movement
can become. Tie your cause to the church—to Christian stewardship."

I responded by saying, "What? I thought you said
we shouldn't talk financial needs." He told me I didn't
understand stewardship. People usually err by limiting
stewardship to dollars, he declared, but this is not biblical.

Dr. Endress then spent about twenty or thirty minutes discussing the biblical meaning of stewardship.
We are not stewards of money and wealth, he said, but

of the gospel. When I accept Jesus as Lord and Savior I become a new person. At that moment he entrusts the gospel to me and I become God's spokesperson. The task and mission of the church and its members are to continue the work Christ began. Time, abilities, and wealth are tools to build God's kingdom. Church colleges, Dr. Endress concluded, are to help young people discover who they are in Christ. The greatest opportunity in the world is to help young people become what God wants them to be. This is the dream and vision people want to be a part of.

I had never heard anyone speak of stewardship in this way! I left his office with a new challenge, a new vision, a new direction and commitment for my life. Another massive gate began to turn on a small hinge!

This ninety-minute visit changed the direction of my life! It caused me to do extensive reading, Bible study, reflection, and testing with others. Little did I realize then that I would be growing with these ideas for the next thirty-three years.

Found—A New Approach in the West!

Our family returned to Kansas July 1, 1957, to find the financial situation as we had left it. I settled into my business manager's role with joy, eager to test with our congregations some of the stewardship approaches suggested by Dr. Endress.

I shared the stewardship ideas with the Hesston College board of overseers, with the new president, Roy Roth, and later with the new president, Tilman Smith. All gave enthusiastic support to experimenting with the new direction. We would tie our cause to a cause bigger than we: continuing the work Christ began.

At that time (1957), our churches west of the Mississippi River were in five geographic clusters called district conferences. I found every opportunity I could to speak at the annual district conference meeting and at the individual congregations. I proposed that our Western churches begin to teach stewardship from the new perspective—mobilizing all of our human gifts and resources to continue the work Christ began. I spoke about the tools given to us for this ministry and the importance of demonstrating our life in Christ by the effective use of our time, abilities, and money. I spoke about biblical "firstfruits" as an individual giving guide for each family to follow.

I suggested that our congregations would be more efficient and effective if they pooled their financial resources through a unified plan called a program budget. Together we worked out per-member congregational goals for each agency of the church. And, you know, the plan began to work!

The new approach to teaching stewardship helped our churches accept a unified distribution system for biblical firstfruits giving. Contributions increased significantly and Hesston College finances improved. No longer was it necessary to travel house-to-house to pick up the college's gifts. Each district conference treasurer sent our share to the college once each quarter. We received more contributions with less expense than before. It was a wonderful change!

Churches in Illinois heard about the work of our churches in the West, and during the 1959-60 school year I shared our experiences with a number of congregations in that state. Goshen College, in Indiana, was interested in our unified approach too. President Paul Mininger invited me to the college faculty retreat to share our story. At that time Goshen College was still involved with the traditional house-to-house "tin cup" approach, and they were looking for a better way. Later President Mininger wrote:

> The proposal of Hesston College to help all congregations face their total financial obligations to all aspects of the church's program is the most significant development in church financing in our brotherhood during the past 50 years.[1]

During this time our national church leadership in the East was hearing reports about our Western ways. The Mennonite General Conference executive secretaries, Paul Erb and later A. J. Metzler, made many inquiries and expressed interest in our new approach. During the early winter months of 1961 they invited me to fill a new position created in the church called Secretary of Stewardship.

This was a surprise. It required a move for our family from Kansas to our church headquarters, then located at Scottdale, Pennsylvania. It meant closing one chapter in my life and beginning a new career. I was 38 years old at the time. We had four children. We hadn't planned to move.

Our family sought counsel and prayed for guidance. Could a layperson lead the church in such an important movement? I asked myself. All of our trusted friends gave us encouragement to try. In the spring months of 1961, we answered yes.

Leaving Hesston was not easy. Our closest friends were there, as were many of our relatives. Our older son was just ready to enter high school. This had been home for 15 significant years of our lives.

---

1. From Mary Miller, *A Pillar of Cloud: The Story of Hesston College 1909-59* (Mennonite Press, North Newton, Kans., 1959), p. 61.

Growing with a Conviction for Stewardship

Our family arrived in Scottdale, Pennsylvania, the last week in July 1961. The Mennonite Publishing House building also housed the headquarters of our Mennonite Church. In our suite of offices worked the Mennonite General Board executive secretary, the youth secretary, the Commission for Christian Education, and now the new stewardship secretary. The Mennonite Church was loosely organized at the top. Our national General Conference met biennially, while each of the seventeen district conferences met annually. We had a membership roll of about 90,000 members in the United States and Canada, and about 900 congregations. We were a small denomination with a big mission.

In my new position I had no continuing program to pick up. The General Board of the church gave me a free and supportive hand in designing and testing new programs. To broaden my horizons I attended the spring meeting of the Department of Stewardship of the National Council of Churches. All major denominations of the United States and Canada were present. Here I learned how other denominational groups approached stewardship issues. With the help of Director T. K. Thompson, I saw that the theological approach of the Lutheran and the Presbyterian stewardship models was nearest to what our Mennonites would accept. I came away with a good theological bibliography to expand my reading and study.

Since there was no continuing program to manage when I began work in August, I had abundant time to study, read, reflect, and dream how to approach stewardship within our tradition. I bought a new wide-margin study Bible and made extensive comments on all the passages I studied. I underlined and commented on hundreds of stewardship passages in the margins. Whenever I read a book with good interpretive comments on a Scripture reference, I underlined the Scripture references and transferred the summary comments to the margins of my "stewardship Bible." After thirty-three years, that study Bible is certainly a rich resource for me now.

During those early days it was important that we develop a long-range denominational strategy for the new stewardship program. The General Board of the church approved the formation of a lay stewardship council made up of persons appointed from each of the seventeen district conferences of the United States and Canada. The council first met in the fall of 1961. The group was enthusiastic about the possibilities. They advised that we select a core of pilot congregations to test ideas and answer questions. For instance, would the "every-member commitment" work in the Mennonite Church? Would some of the more conservative Eastern conferences accept the unified program budget? Would ministers accept the idea that we are stewards of the gospel?

The pilot congregations were selected. Ideas and procedures were tested. Some ideas didn't survive; others were modified. Eventually the pilot congregations developed a guidebook called *Stewardship for Mission*, to begin the new stewardship teaching program.

Nelson Kauffman—pastor, church planter, and evangelist—and I explored how some of the other denominations were teaching their pastors this new understanding and theology of stewardship. We developed our own study manual and invited the pastors and lay leaders of a district conference to a two-day regional

Stewardship Training Institute. Here we asked each small study group to write its own definition of Christian stewardship. All the definitions were similar. "Christian stewardship is a person's grateful, obedient response to God's redeeming love, expressed through the use of all of our resources for the continuation of Christ's mission in the world."[2] It was amazing that after only two days of Bible study persons would move this far in their understanding of stewardship. When they came to the meeting, the majority thought we were going to talk about raising funds for the church!

For the record, I should point out that about this time the General Conference Mennonite Church appointed Pastor Lester Janzen to be its stewardship secretary. The two of us worked closely together in developing a workable plan for both of our Mennonite traditions.

Eventually, the long-range plan for the strategy of teaching stewardship evolved into an organized program.

First, we began a series of two-day stewardship institutes for a cluster of congregations within each conference district. Ministers and key lay leaders would attend. No meeting would have more than 40 to 50 persons present.

Second, we followed institutes with an eight-hour, one-day training session on Stewardship for Mission. During this day we outlined a several-year congregational teaching plan involving preaching, gift discernment, calling and assigning persons with special gifts. The teaching also covered annual program planning, financing (including the every-member commitment),

---

2. From *Stewardship for Mission in the Local Congregation* (Mennonite Publishing House, Scottdale, Pa., rev. ed., 1966), p. 12.

interpreting the world program of the church in an exciting way, and helping members to feel they were a dynamic part of Christ's mission for the church.

Third, we prepared a speakers' bureau of qualified stewardship persons, and distributed it to pastors so they could call on these resource persons to reinforce whatever stewardship step the congregation was working through.

Fourth, we wrote news releases for the church press whenever something significant in stewardship happened. We published the stories of good experiences in a congregation to encourage other congregations who were hesitant to move into the program.

Fifth, we gave progress reports at all district conferences or ministers' meetings.

Finally, for special study conferences, we brought in resource leaders from other Christian traditions to reinforce our own teaching. These persons were T. K. Thompson and Nordan Murphy of the stewardship department of the National Council of Churches, Henry Endress of the Lutheran Church, and John Thompson Peters of the Presbyterian Church.

This long-range program seemed to work well. While the plan was not completely free of criticism, most congregations did accept the basic elements of the various proposals and steps. From 1961 to 1971 all but three conferences moved into a unified distribution plan. This was a big step forward for our Mennonite tradition.

A Side Step and Detour

In the fall of 1966 Edith and I had two children in college and the prospect of two more entering college soon. We were confronted with overwhelming family financial needs.

About that time the local public school district asked me to be the associate superintendent of schools for business and federal programs. What should we do now? The additional salary would double our income and solve our cash problem. Also, Edith began teaching again about this time. We sought counsel from some of our trusted friends in the Scottdale, Pennsylvania, area. Each felt we should accept the new offer. The General Board of the church felt the stewardship program was "off and running," so I accepted the new job—my first position in a nonchurch agency.

Back to Higher Education

Late in 1970 the Goshen College Board of Overseers elected J. Lawrence Burkholder as president. During the spring months of 1971, as he was assembling his new administrative team, he asked me to join him as his development officer responsible for college relations. This was another difficult decision. Another massive gate was soon to turn on the small hinge of decision. I believed deeply in the church college as a place out of which to form church and community leadership. But I had been in my public school position only four and one-half years. Was it too early to move? Was my work completed there?

On July 5, 1971, we moved to Goshen, Indiana, to begin another chapter in our lives.

Would a biblical approach to stewardship work in college development? I knew it worked 13 years earlier at Hesston College. But there we were working only at congregational support. Now I was faced with motivating the financial support of all publics.

Alumni, parents, business and industry, faculty and staff, friends, congregations, and foundations responded generously. During the next 15-year period, these groups increased their total annual giving to all funds at an average compounded rate of 10.45 percent per year. The accumulated total dollars contributed during this 15-year period was $31.5 million. In addition, in 1986 we completed a four-year deferred giving endowment campaign in which these same persons committed an additional $20 million through their wills, charitable trusts, annuities, and other forms of deferred gifts.

How did this happen? Was it just "hype" and public relations techniques? No, there was more behind the response than that! President Burkholder described the cause of Goshen College as one that is uncommon. He spoke and wrote extensively how and why Goshen College is different from other colleges; how our Christian, value-oriented faculty approach the learning and growing process in youth. He explained why it's important for faculty to integrate Christian faith and life and how faith values are united with learning and careers. He showed how a liberal arts education and cross-cultural overseas experience prepare a young student to be a global citizen.

Because he and others articulated our mission so clearly and in such a compelling way, donors responded. They wanted to feel they were personally needed to perpetuate the values that had guided each of them through the years.

Earlier in this chapter I described how Henry Endress told me that people give to a mission, to dreams and to visions. Helping donors feel they are an integral part of a mission which prepares youth for a life of service in our communities is motivating!

• • •

In July of 1986 I reached that magic age of retirement. Things are more relaxed now, as I reflect on a life of service to the church. This has been my faith story. What I speak and what I write in the next ten chapters comes out of this pilgrimage. When I was a young man interested in entering business, the last thing that would have entered my mind was the story I have told in this chapter. The "massive gates of circumstance" did indeed turn on a series of small hinges!

It is my conviction that the Christian mission is to continue the work Christ began. Furthermore, the church's mission will be ineffective unless Christians focus their time, their abilities, and their wealth to accomplish this common task. As leaders we stand between two churches—the one we have known and the one toward which we are heading. The way we teach stewardship in our congregations will be a major factor in determining the future of that church we are now facing.

2

Stewards of the Gospel

Matthew 25:14-30
Luke 7:36-48

EVERY PERSON in the Christian church has a perception of the meaning of stewardship. Most people equate the word with either the management of money, the church offering, or congregational concern about low cash flow. It is not uncommon to hear a pastor introduce the Sunday offering by saying, "We will now worship in stewardship."

Equating stewardship with giving has paid off. Look at our world missions, our church institutions, our variety of church and community affairs, even our church bureaucracy. The monetary perception of stewardship has motivated people to give to a plethora of organizations. Some people even use these concepts to justify free enterprise as God's favorite economy!

I have frequently said that a vibrant church and a giving church go hand in hand. And doesn't the Scripture say, "For where your treasure is, there your heart will be also" (Matt. 6:21)?

People refer to stewardship in other ways too. The procrastinator might call himself a "poor steward of time." Or a person opposed to a new program suggested for the congregation might argue that the proposal is "poor stewardship."

But do these uses reflect a truly biblical understanding of stewardship? Are stewardship, money, and benevolences as closely related as we think they are? Let's take a fresh look at the Bible and allow the Scriptures to speak for themselves.

Meaning of the Term

The New Testament uses a series of Greek words from which our English words *steward, stewardship,* and *ambassador* are derived.

Greek Word	English Meaning
Oikos	Home dwelling, household, temple.
Nomos	Administration, management, parceling out (especially food and the grazing of animals).
Oikonomos	The overseer, administrator, fiscal agent, governor (usually translated *steward* or *ambassador* in the NT). *Oikonomoi* is the plural form of *oikonomos*.
Oikonomia	The administration of an estate, a household, or a temple (usually translated *stewardship* in the NT).

In the biblical sense, a steward (*oikonomos*) is a person who is in charge of a household or an estate. The administration of this responsibility is stewardship (*oikonomia*). The steward is not the owner, but he or she has been left in charge of the management (*oikonomia*) while the owner has gone away. The owner holds the steward responsible for the administration of the estate (Matt 25:14-30). The steward buys and sells goods and binds and looses administrative agreements (Matt. 16:19; 18:18; John 20:23), always for the benefit of the owner. Eventually the owner will return home to check on the management (*oikonomia*) of the steward (*oikonomos*). (See Luke 19:12-27.)

On some occasions in the Bible the word *ambassador* is the term used for steward (*oikonomos*). An ambassador is one nation's top representative to another nation. He is powerful, yet commissioned to be a true and responsible representative of the home nation. He knows there will be an accounting and reporting period on his administration (*oikonomia*) each time he returns home (2 Cor. 5:6-21).

There are other meanings of these two terms— *steward* and *stewardship*—in the Scriptures. Our words *manager, management, economics, buy, sell, profitability,* and *investment* all fall within the contextual use of the Greek words *oikonomos* and *oikonomia*.

When Jesus uses the two words, his stories have economic implications, but one always hears a deeper meaning through the stories' metaphors. When Paul uses the two words, he is *never* speaking of dollars and cents or the economics of a situation, though he does use the words *steward* and *stewardship* in various discussions of the entrustment of great worth (Titus 1:7-10; 1 Cor. 4:1-5; Eph. 3:1-13; 1 Pet. 4:10-11).

What is it, then, that is entrusted to Christians to

manage? And who is the absentee landlord who has gone to a far country?

A few words will put Jesus' metaphors into place. We are entrusted with the gospel, the kingdom of God, the plan of redemption. We become managers for God, his representatives, his voices. This is our stewardship (*oikonomia*). We become stewards of the gospel.

In some denominations, the words *disciple* and *discipleship* are important. The Greek word for disciple literally means follower, imitator, servant, one who learns from a teacher or rabbi. Becoming a disciple is important to the dedicated Christian.

When I become a steward of the gospel, I'm the chief executive officer, God's spokesperson, God's manager. When God entrusts to me the gospel, he uses my voice and my personality to communicate his message. If I'm unfaithful, the kingdom falls into bad repute. The responsibility of a steward is greater than the responsibility of a disciple!

In contrast to other Christian traditions, the Mennonite tradition has emphasized discipleship more than stewardship. Both concepts are central to Christian people.

Teachings from Jesus, Paul, John, and Peter

Early in Jesus' ministry he said, "I have come that they may have life, and have it to the full" (John 10:10). And, "Your Father has been pleased to give you the kingdom" (Luke 12:32). Jesus spent the remaining three years of his life explaining and interpreting the kingdom of God and how each believer participates in it.

Most of Jesus' teaching came through stories. He left

the *interpretations* of the stories to those who took him seriously.

The parable of the talents (Matt. 25:14-30) is a familiar kingdom story. As a boy, I thought our Sunday school teachers equated *talent* with *ability*. When asked to do something, I might have humbly responded, "Oh, I'm just a one-talent person. Why don't you ask Mary or John?" What a mistaken interpretation that was! Had we remembered what happened to the one-talent person at the end of the parable, none of us would have claimed that distinction!

The talents parable helps us understand biblical stewardship. Here Jesus uses the image of *oikonomos* and *oikonomia*. The owner of a household was leaving for a far country, so he called together his servants (*oikonomoi*) to transfer the management (*oikonomia*) of his property to them. To one he gave five measures of property, to another, three, and to another, one. After a long time the owner returned to check on the management of the servants. Each was rewarded according to the faithfulness of his or her management performance.

What might our contemporary interpretation of this story be? And what did Jesus mean when he said the kingdom is like this (Matt. 25:14)?

Perhaps Jesus was the person leaving on a journey. Before leaving, he called his followers around him and distributed to each the responsibility to continue the kingdom work while he was gone. To one he gave five measures of gospel, to another, three, and to another, one. Some faithfully carried on the Christian's responsibility of modeling the gospel and the kingdom—the five- and the three-talent people. Others were faithful at first, but didn't work at it diligently. Eventually they lost their faith. You might say the one-talent person became interested in other interests and buried the one measure of gospel he had received.

Jesus said men and women experiencing the gospel should be assertive with the talents allotted them. We should strive to continue his work or we will lose the faith we have. Many of Jesus' stories hold up faithfulness and obedience as our primary responsibilities. God calls us to be faithful and obedient more than God calls us to be successful.

In Matthew 13 Jesus gives us a series of short parables that interpret the way we are to respond to the gospel. "A farmer went out to sow" (v. 3) teaches that we are to sow and share the gospel wherever we go. "The kingdom of heaven is like a mustard seed" (vv. 31-32) compares the gospel to a small seed that takes root slowly but grows into a mighty tree where birds find refuge. The responsible and mature Christian is to be a refuge for those seeking faith.

"The kingdom of heaven is like yeast" (v. 33) suggests that we allow the gospel (yeast) to affect fully our lives. "The kingdom of heaven is like treasure hidden in a field" (v. 44) tells of a man discovering a box while cultivating his field. The digger immediately knows he has found valuable buried treasure, so he sells everything he has to buy the field. The gospel is like this, Jesus says. When we discover it, we will devote our lives to its care and administration.

The apostle Paul discusses the same stewardship *(oikonomia)* concepts that Jesus so clearly communicates. We have been "approved by God to be entrusted with the gospel," he writes (1 Thess. 2:4). "For we are God's fellow workers [*oikonomoi*]; you are God's field, God's building" (1 Cor. 3:9). In these two passages we have the dignity of being called co-workers. Paul continues, "So then, men ought to regard us as servants of Christ and as those entrusted with the secret things of God. Now it is required that those who have been given a trust must prove faithful" (1 Cor. 4:1-2).

In 2 Corinthians Paul describes stewards as new persons with new motivations, fully responsible to use their time, abilities, and possessions for the advancement of the gospel. Stewards are, he says, "Christ's ambassadors, as though God were making his appeal through us" (5:20). As God's ambassadors, we are important representatives of the kingdom. God communicates his message through us.

In Ephesians Paul gives us yet another stewardship message. He writes, "For it is by grace you have been saved, through faith. . . . It is the gift of God. . . . For we are God's workmanship, created in Christ Jesus to do good works" (Eph. 2:8-10).

And finally, in 1 Peter 4:10-11, we read, "Each one should use whatever gift he has received to serve others, faithfully administering [literally, as good *stewards* of—*oikonomoi*] God's grace in its various forms. If anyone speaks, he should do it as one speaking the very words of God. If anyone serves, he should do it with the strength God provides, so that in all things God may be praised through Jesus Christ." Though Peter is writing to the scattered Christians of Asia Minor, he might be talking to us today, appealing to us to remember that we are God's spokespersons and stewards.

Christians have the responsibility to be God's voice and to be his service agents. This includes wise use of relationships, prayer, influence, time, talent, treasure, and all the forms of God's grace showered upon us. Our mission is to continue the work Christ began!

Stewardship Begins with Receiving

In 1957 I heard Paul Tillich declare one day, "Stewardship begins with receiving, not with giving." He explained that the Christian must first discover and receive Jesus Christ as Lord and Savior, experience forgiveness and redemption, and form a new identity with the community of faith. At that point the Christian has something to share with others.

To illustrate, Tillich used the moving story of the Pharisee and the sinful woman (Luke 7:36-48). I will tell the story as I remember Paul Tillich did in 1957.

Simon the Pharisee invited Jesus to lunch one day, a natural act of courtesy for a religious Pharisee. As Jesus entered Simon's house, a sinful woman followed him through the door. She knelt beside him and began to weep. She wept so much, in fact, she washed Jesus' feet with her tears! Then she took down her hair and dried his feet. Earlier that morning she had withdrawn her life savings from the Savings and Loan and purchased an alabaster box of precious ointment. In devotion to Jesus, she broke the box and anointed Jesus' feet.

This act seemed utterly wasteful to Simon, though he didn't have the courage to criticize Jesus for permitting such a display. Instead he thought to himself, "If this man were a prophet, he would know what sort of woman is touching him, for she is a sinner."

Jesus interpreted Simon's perplexed and disgusted glances and said to him, "Simon, I have something to say to you!" Jesus then told a story. Two persons owed a certain man money, one $500 and the other $50. Because neither could pay, the creditor canceled both debts. "Which one of the two men will love the creditor the most?" Jesus asked. Simon thought a while and then answered, "The one, I suppose, to whom he forgave more." Jesus responded quickly, saying, "That's right."

Then Jesus turned to Simon and recited to him the significant events of the preceding fifteen minutes. He reminded Simon that *he* should have been the person washing Jesus' feet. He replayed how the sinful woman experienced forgiveness and completely dedicated her life to Jesus. "He who is forgiven little, loves little," Jesus said. By implication, the woman first received generously then gave generously!

Tillich closed by repeating, "Stewardship begins with receiving, not with giving." He raised one open hand to symbolize the receiving of forgiveness and redemption. The other hand he stretched out immediately in front of him, palm open, symbolizing the giving hand. He said a number of times, "receiving . . . giving . . . receiving . . . giving," motioning with the appropriate hand as he emphasized each word.

This passage from Luke 7 is one of the more profound stewardship passages in the Bible. For some, the idea of sharing the gospel is not motivating, because they have never received forgiveness. Like Simon, they have nothing to share. But the woman voluntarily and completely reordered her life and dedicated all her personal resources for the kingdom. This is exactly what Paul means when he speaks about becoming a new creation (2 Cor. 5:17).

John says it clearly, too: "We love because he first loved us" (1 John 4:19). God made the first move in the stewardship act. He gave us Jesus and redemption. This is *love*, John says. If we accept Christ's redeeming love, we can respond through loving and redeeming relationships with others.

One's interest in the church is in direct relationship

to the depths of one's experience with Christ. If my experience is shallow, I will respond like Simon. If my experience with Christ is similar to the sinful woman's, I become a new creation.

We usually begin our stewardship teaching by referring to the large financial needs facing our congregation, church board, or agency. Instead, we should begin by helping our people see who they are in Christ. We should be showing them the new opportunities that grow out of that experience. When I experience the joy of sins forgiven, as did the sinful woman, I enthusiastically volunteer my skills and financial resources so others can grow into this experience also.

The Arts Can Communicate Too

Some years ago a popular musical played on Broadway, *The Sound of Music*. It was the story of a music-loving postulant from an abbey in Austria who becomes the governess in the home of a widowed naval captain. In the musical, the governess falls in love with the children's father, Baron Von Trapp. One evening she sings to the baron a love song that communicates the same perceptions Paul Tillich spoke of when he discussed receiving and giving. Maria sings about a bell not being a bell until it rings, a song not being a song until it is sung, and love not being love until one gives it away.

A bell in the church steeple is not a bell until it begins to ring, reverberating across the countryside. A song is not a song until the members of the congregation sing the words with their lips and voices. Likewise, God's love was not fully expressed until it was given on the cross for humanity. Love is not love until you give it away.

Many church hymnals have the classic hymn, "When I Survey the Wondrous Cross." In verse 4, the final line picks up the same love theme: "Love so amazing, so divine, demands my soul, my life, my all."

When a person receives this kind of forgiveness there is revival! It's surprising to many people that revival can come through an understanding of Christian stewardship.

Stewardship Defined

Stewardship is the grateful, obedient response of the whole person continuing the work Christ began. It is the point where the vitality and the genuineness of the Christian experience become visible.

Jesus and the apostles Paul, John, and Peter all confirm this understanding.

3

The Christian's Grateful and Obedient Response

Ephesians 2:8-10
2 Corinthians 5:16-20
Luke 19:1-10

IN CHAPTER 2, we looked at biblical stewardship as the management responsibility of a major trust—the gospel. Having received the trust, the Christian gratefully and obediently responds by dedicating his or her resources to communicating the good news to others. The New Testament reduced to a short mission statement might read, "To continue the work Christ began."

In this chapter we look at the tools Christians use in their stewardship (*oikonomia*) of the gospel. At birth, each of us receives an allotment of time, intellect, and ability. Each of us is born into a material world of personal property, real estate, and money. We are free moral agents and we can use these tools to achieve our personal goals.

Consider the carpenter. He is certainly a free person, but he has a well-defined purpose: to build. When he comes on the job, you don't expect him to spend time sharpening the saw or keeping the hammer polished. You expect him to have sharp tools and to use them to get down to work. If he doesn't do the job well, you look for a new carpenter.

Now the tools each of us have are like the carpenter's tools. They are important, to be sure. In our youth we study and train, sharpening our tools and preparing them for use. But we don't expect to spend a lifetime in school. Eventually we must use our abilities, our time, and our resources for a specific purpose.

Remember the passage from Ephesians 2? Paul writes, "For it is by grace you have been saved, through faith. . . . It is the gift of God. . . . For we are God's workmanship, created in Christ Jesus to do good works" (Eph. 2:8-10).

Created to do good works. What a marvelous directive for the Christian! It is true we are free moral agents, but when we become the new creations Paul speaks about in 2 Corinthians 5, we begin to use our tools for the advancement and development of Christ's kingdom. Paul says it this way:

> So from now on we regard no one from a worldly point of view. . . . Therefore, if anyone is in Christ, he is a new creation; the old has gone, the new has come! All this is from God, who reconciled us to himself through Christ and gave us the ministry of reconciliation. . . . We are therefore Christ's ambassadors, as though God were making his appeal through us.
>
> (2 Cor. 5:16-20)

Christians have accepted this view around the world. But while we teach the importance of time and the development of our abilities, we scarcely mention the importance of the third tool: wealth. We have done little teaching in the church on the positive use of wealth and its importance in continuing Christ's work. In fact, we have separated what God intended to be together—his mission and the economic resources needed to achieve it.

We read so much in Christian literature on the evils of wealth that we find it difficult to contemplate its *importance* in the hands of dedicated Christians. The church develops elaborate service programs around the world. We train people for service and ask them to dedicate twenty-five to forty years of their time and abilities. But we fail to support them with the financial resources necessary to make those programs fully effective.

The story of Zacchaeus (Luke 19:1-10) illustrates the positive use of money in a biblical context. Zacchaeus, you probably remember, was a tax collector. He was rich and spent his money in a conspicuous and irritating way. But one day he witnessed the presence and mission of Jesus during his lunch hour, and he experienced redemption. In grateful obedience he declared, "Look, Lord! Here and now I give half of my possessions to the poor, and if I have cheated anybody out of anything, I will pay back four times the amount" (Luke 19:8). What a marvelous response! Formerly, Zacchaeus had contributed to the injustice of society. Now he was using money to correct, to some degree, the injustice he had had a part in perpetuating.

The Zacchaeus story illustrates well Paul Tillich's statement that "stewardship begins with receiving, not with giving." Zacchaeus would never have responded to social problems had fund-raisers approached him saying, "Zac, we have this need. How much can you give?" He first needed a vision of who he was in

Christ and what he could become. With his vision corrected, his generous response was voluntary!

Joining Creation and Redemption

This chapter has introduced the triad of tools given to us at birth: time, ability, and wealth. Now we need to bring together the two gift themes of the Scripture: redemption and creation. Each theme is ineffective without the other.

I was a grown man before it dawned on me that the entire mid-America section is one huge river system made up of the Mississippi and Missouri Rivers. The total system, including tributaries, includes about 14,000 miles of river. The two rivers alone are 3,892 miles long. The Mississippi flows out of Itasca Lake in northern Minnesota, where it is ten feet wide and about two feet deep. By the time it reaches the Gulf of Mexico, it is well over a mile wide—a great river.

The biggest major river joining the Mississippi is the Missouri. It begins on the northwestern slopes of the Yellowstone National Park and flows across Montana, North Dakota, South Dakota, Nebraska, and a corner of Kansas. At Kansas City, it turns east and flows across the state of Missouri, merging with the Mississippi in St. Louis.

If you stood a mile south of the confluence of these two great bodies in St. Louis, it would be impossible to take two gallons of water from the river and say, "This gallon came from Yellowstone and the other from Minnesota." At the confluence the waters churn and the two rivers become one.

Note the following diagrams.

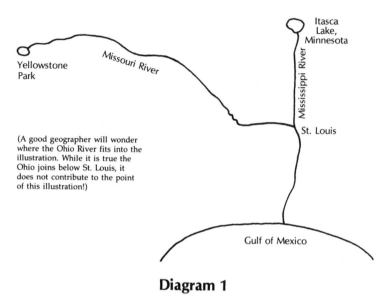

Diagram 1

The Mississippi River system can illustrate how two streams of thought and experience can be merged into one.

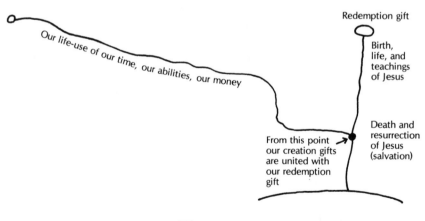

Diagram 2

The Christian's story begins with the redemption theme in the birth, life, and teachings of Jesus. With Christ's death and resurrection, the plan reaches its climax. In fact, Paul becomes so excited about the centrality of this message that in 1 Corinthians 15:17 he says, "If Christ has not been raised, your faith is futile."

Shortly after the resurrection, of course, Jesus ascended into heaven and left his followers the task of continuing his mission. (This is the absentee landlord idea spoken of in Chapter 2.)

Now enter the creation theme. I am a free moral agent, born to use my gifts in my own way. One day, as I flow along the river of life, I am confronted with redemption. I accept God's plan for my life. I become a new person. I now reorient my goals and purpose. I use the gifts of creation to continue the gift of redemption. The two themes of the Bible (redemption and creation) become one, as the Mississippi and the Missouri rivers become one below the confluence in St. Louis. The steward (*oikonomos*) the New Testament speaks about moves into his or her stewardship (*oikonomia*) responsibilities.

When a person discovers who he or she is in Christ, the response of the sinful woman (Luke 7) or the response of Zacchaeus (Luke 19) is natural, voluntary, obedient, joyful. This is our stewardship, expressed so well in the following hymn:

God, Whose Giving[1]

God, whose giving knows no ending,
All our life is from thy store:

Nature's wonder, Jesus' wisdom,
Costly cross, grave's shattered door.
Gifted by thee, turn we to thee,
Offering up ourselves in praise;
Thankful song shall rise forever;
Gracious donor of our days.

Skills and time are ours for pressing
Toward the goals of Christ, thy Son:
Men at peace in health and freedom,
Races joined, the church made one.
Now direct our daily labor,
Lest we strive for self alone;
Born with talents make us servants
Fit to answer at thy throne.

Treasure, too, thou hast entrusted,
Gain through powers thy grace conferred;
Ours to use for home and kindred,
And to spread the gospel Word.
Open wide our hands in sharing,
As we heed Christ's ageless call,
Healing, teaching, and reclaiming,
Serving thee who lovest all.

Lend thy joy in all our giving,
Let it light our pilgrim way;
From the dark of anxious keeping,
Loose us into generous day.
Then when years on earth are over,
Rich toward thee and fellow man,
Lord, fulfill beyond our dreaming
All our steward life began.

Amen.

4

The Christian Family and Its Decisions

John 21:1-17
Galatians 5:16-25

CHAPTERS 2 and 3 presented the theology of stewardship. Now we bring that biblical understanding into the twentieth century. Christianity is to be lived on the road—between Sundays, not just in the sanctuary. In fact, for Christianity to be authentic, it must be lived in the midst of the hard facts of life—in the home, factory, school, office, shop, club, farm, market —wherever people are.

We live in a complex world of joy and depression, success and failure, wealth and poverty. We always live in the hope that tomorrow will be better. We are confronted with hundreds of decisions every day: questions of lifestyle, career choices, management problems, guidance of children, and personal relationships.

Several years ago a researcher discovered the average person will have 1,540 significant messages requiring a decision beamed at him every day. Whether we

47

make a hundred or 1,540 decisions, we need to ask the questions: Why do I do what I do? What are the influences in my life that control my destiny and faith-related decisions? Considering that Christ has made me a steward of the gospel, how does that belief affect my decision-making process?

Values Control Our Decisions

The word *value* is commonly used in this decade. A definition might be, "That intangible worth I assign to an experience, a belief, a position, or a goal and for which I am willing to spend time, energy, or money to experience."

Values are powerful engines of human action. They determine good or bad behavior, what is beautiful or ugly, what is profitable or unprofitable, what is useful or useless, what makes us feel good or bad about a decision, what is in fashion or out of fashion, what is moral or immoral. The list could go on, but my point is clear: Our values are important and need to be examined.

Values are learned, not inborn. We develop them through instruction, observation, and use. Sometimes values are *caught* more than taught—perhaps through the body language of a parent, a role model, or hero.

Finally, we prioritize our values (see *Diagram 3*). Some are more important than others. Christian values we respect are love, peace, justice, compassion, forgiveness, self-control, gentleness, and meekness (Gal. 5:22-23). These are the gifts of the Spirit the Bible encourages us to nourish. We place them above economic expediences, above personal comfort and interest.

Values are something like software in our computers. After the software disk is in place, the computer can sort through multiple keyboard inputs, always printing the right answers by sorting through the minutia fed into the computer through the operator and keyboard. You see, values are placed subliminally (as software) in our brain. We are confronted with scores of decisions each day. It is the values (software) that direct the printout (decisions)! Change values and we make different decisions.

Values are the constants of our existence. Like navigational aids or fixed points of reference, they keep us from wandering aimlessly from one crisis to another. They give us hope for transcending the constant change and turmoil of our times.

We can prioritize our values. The following diagram expresses this concept.

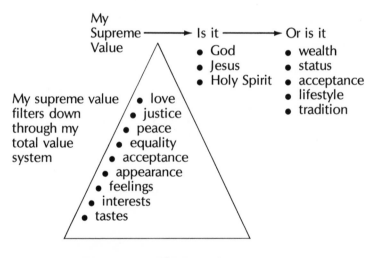

Diagram 3

Let's assume I need to buy a pair of dress shoes sometime soon. I know I want a pair of oxfords and I prefer leather soles and uppers to plastic. These are decisions I make according to personal preference and comfort. When I actually make the shopping trip I choose a day other than Sunday. Oh, I'm not the kind to think God will condemn me if I make a Sunday purchase! But because of my reverence for the Lord's Day, I schedule my free time so Sunday is a day of worship and rest. The other six days are for work and other personal matters.

You see, in this simple story I have established priorities. Because I have an active belief and commitment to God, I allow God's Word to direct me. The commitment to God as my supreme value filters down through the decision-making process, affecting all decisions I make.

Higher on the triangle I select other decisions, such as college attendance, career choice, spouse selection, and faith issues. These choices are more complex and will affect my lifestyle. Their importance is obvious.

Now the major question is, "What supreme value affects every decision I make?" Many readers will likely respond, "God is my supreme value." That's right! Yet another set of supreme values sits at the top of the triangle. For instance, I may go to church on Sunday, sing the hymns and listen attentively to the sermon. However, as I enter the road of decision-making on Monday morning, all too often another set of well-established secular values begins to take over. The Sunday experience is only ritual. Monday is where the action begins!

From Chapter 1 you know I have spent many years on a church college campus. I have often observed that acceptance by one's peer group is very important to young people. Some will lay aside their home and church teachings when they come to campus. And certainly we who are older aren't much different! The lure of secular values is compelling to all of us.

It's difficult to know what a person does believe. The best guide is to observe the decisions he or she makes. Psychologists tell us people will always be true to that "inner something" that governs behavior.

Some years ago a national business magazine presented an article on business ethics and moral standards. It was the author's opinion that the morality of a company begins with top management. The writer quoted company presidents speaking about the importance of guiding standards and work codes. Later, those same presidents were disciplined for accepting kickbacks on some of their corporate purchases. The article closed with this statement: "Don't ask persons what they believe, just observe the decisions they make!"

A Typical Family Decision (A Case Story)

The following story is fictional. I wrote it in the first person to help readers identify with similar situations in their own lives. Consider it a case study on decision-making:

I'm a lay person working as the chief development officer for a church college. The job has its normal pressures. Long hours and evening and weekend assignments are normal. One Saturday morning, as my wife, Edith, and I awakened, we discovered this was a free day. We were delighted. We began to make plans.

It was the middle of July. I was to mow the grass early in the morning, then take the children to their music lessons at about eleven o'clock. This would permit Edith to do some of her normal Saturday work without the interruption of "taxi" duty. During the afternoon I planned to paint the lawn chairs. Toward late afternoon I would go out into the woods to begin cutting firewood for the fall and winter.

Our work plan began right on schedule. About 9:10, as I was mowing grass, Edith called to say I had a telephone call. "Oh, no," I said. "Surely I don't have to go into the college." My fears were unfounded.

It was Bill Moss, the Sunday school superintendent, calling to ask me to teach class on Sunday morning because our regular teacher was ill. I told him, "Bill, I know you think I should, but I'm home so rarely on Saturday, and today we have planned family activities all day. I don't have time to prepare the lesson. Why don't you call Joe or Sarah? They're capable teachers. They both have five talents and I'm only a one-talent guy!"

Bill laughed at my one-talent reference and said he would try someone else.

I scarcely got the mower started when Edith called me with another phone call. I came to the house wondering, "Why don't they leave me alone?" When the caller turned out to be Phil Dooner, my mood changed. Phil was the president of the largest bank in the community. We had been encouraging the bank to make a gift to the college, but Phil was always aloof. This morning, however, he was friendly and warm.

"Dan isn't this a perfect day!" he said.

I answered, "Yes, it's great for mowing."

Phil countered, "Dan, you need a break. How about joining me at the golf course about eleven o'clock? Don Peachey of the Western Steel Company and Joe Gratzer from Allied Rubber will meet us there and we'll have a foursome."

I hesitated a moment, then said, "Oh, Phil, Edith

and I had planned to—" and I began to share with Phil our family plans for the day. But suddenly it dawned on me what an opportunity this was—to play golf with three of the top leaders of our community. Further, they all had money! I stopped telling Phil of our plans and abruptly said, "Why yeah. That's a great idea. I'll meet the three of you at eleven o'clock!"

I called Edith to the phone and told her about the call. I suggested to her that she could take the children to their music lessons. "We can paint the lawn chairs in August, and we still have several months to cut wood before winter."

Edith smiled knowingly and said, "There are some things that just don't change in you! Why is golf more important to you than the Sunday school class or the family?"

Although the story is fictional, it could have happened in our home. Perhaps the writer is correct. "Don't ask a person what he believes, just observe the decisions he makes." Our individual decisions do have a way of exposing our inner beliefs, commitments, and drives.

Jesus' Story of Supreme Values

There is a fascinating story about Jesus in John 21:1-17. The plot begins after the resurrection. Peter must have thought everything was over, because he called six of his friends to join him in reopening his fishing company. When the six joined him, Peter said, "I am going fishing."

The six responded, "We will go with you." They fished all night, with poor results.

As the sun was coming up, they noticed a figure on

the beach who called out to them saying, "Have you any fish?"

They answered him, "No."

Then the man called to them again, "Cast your nets on the right side of the boat and you will find some." The seven men did this and immediately they caught so many fish the boat nearly sank.

At this point John said to Peter, "It is the Lord!" Peter became so excited that he put on his clothes and told the others they should bring in the boat and the fish. Peter jumped overboard and waded to the shore. After the other men docked the boat, Jesus told them to bring some of their fish over for broiling.

After breakfast Jesus asked Peter a simple question, "Peter, do you love me more than these?" Now, the meaning of *these* is not clear. I have heard some pastors say Jesus was referring to the other disciples. This may be right. But I believe that when Jesus said "these," he made a sweeping motion with one hand toward the fish left on the beach. So he was really asking the question, "Peter, what is going to have first place in your life—your business (symbolized by the fish) or me?" It is the same question I was working with earlier when I wrote, "What is your supreme value?"

In answer to Jesus' question, Peter said, "Yes, Lord, you know that I love you." They repeated this question and answer three times. Finally Peter answered emphatically, "Lord, you know everything; you know that I love you!" And for the third time Jesus repeated softly, "Feed my sheep."

The supreme test of commitment in Jesus' mind was Peter's willingness to put Christ above "these"—his business, his life goals, his status in society. Christ's answer, "Feed my sheep," might be articulated by the apostle James when he writes, "Do not merely listen to the word, and so deceive yourselves. Do what it says. Anyone who listens to the word but does not do what it says is like a man who looks at his face in a mirror and, after looking at himself, goes away and immediately forgets what he looks like" (James 1:22-24).

Jesus' words to Peter are much like those of Paul to the Ephesians. "We are God's workmanship, created in Christ Jesus to do good works, which God prepared in advance for us to do" (Eph. 2:10).

We have been discussing the process of family and individual decision-making. Through our decisions we demonstrate what we believe. By "feeding Christ's sheep" we express our internal faith and Christian experience. Likewise, these acts of voluntary service and obedience stimulate others to be the kinds of persons God wants them to be.

Jesus shared many stories about decisions of supreme value. In Luke 9:59-62, for instance, he invites several persons to follow him. When one man responds, "First let me go and bury my father," Jesus gives a harsh answer, "Let the dead bury their own dead, but you go and proclaim the kingdom of God." To the same invitation another person answers, "First let me go back and say good-by to my family." Jesus gives him a harsh answer too. "No one who puts his hand to the plow and looks back is fit for service in the kingdom of God."

Certainly these strong statements emphasize the importance of defining and identifying our supreme value and commitment. When we are confronted with those 1,540 daily messages requiring decisions, our responses will be consistent with what we say we believe.

It's important that Christian people have a church

community and a support group to which to relate. Just having trusted friends who will walk along beside us is reassuring. Our church support group can help us with consistent teaching, motivation, value identification, and assistance in solving problems. We will say more about this in Chapter 8 when we discuss congregational strategic planning for Christian stewardship.

Finally, let me repeat: If you want to know what a person believes, just observe the decisions he or she makes!

5

The Meaning and Importance of Money

Luke 16:1-15
Matthew 6:19-33
Mark 7:20-23
Romans 1:28-32

A man's treatment of money is the most decisive test of his character—how he makes it and how he spends it. (James M. Moffat, 1870–1944)

Money. 200 proof. Taken straight or mixed with many lovely things, it's the most intoxicating substance known. (David Augsburger)

Money is a miraculous thing. It is your personal energy reduced to portable form and endowed with power you do not possess. It can go where you cannot go; speak languages you cannot speak; lift burdens you cannot touch with your fingers; save lives with which you cannot deal directly.
(Harry Emerson Fosdick, 1878-1969)

THE THIRD TOOL God gave us to use in our stewardship of the gospel is money. Money is much more controversial than time and ability. Because people seldom speak positively about it in the church, we now devote a chapter to its meaning and significance.

Money is a dominant component of our lives, ever present in our thoughts and conversations. Here are four short vignettes to illustrate the point.

Several years ago I was traveling with five other men for several days, criss-crossing states and making fifteen to twenty stops to look at farmland and other assets. From morning until night the talk was about money. In the van, in the restaurant, in the motel room, the conversation ranged from farm prices, stock prices, retirement packages, church budgets, college costs, and third-world needs. Money, money, money!

Recently my wife and I visited a church camp. The month was August, just before school started. Next to our bedroom in the camp lodge were four mothers. The lodge walls were thin, permitting sound to pass through like a sieve. What do mothers of school-age children talk about from ten o'clock until eleven at night in August? The price of school clothing and shoes, low summer earnings, and the cost of outfitting their children with band instruments and athletic gear. Money, money, money!

During the 1960s and 1970s our youth across the nation were restless and rebellious. Hair and clothing styles were foreign to many of us. The youth had a message for us older people, and money and material- istic drives in their parents' generation certainly were a vital part of that message. Money, money, money!

In the early 1980s I was in a Goshen, Indiana, res- taurant for lunch one day. The waitresses behind the counter were talking among themselves with gusto. One waitress in her early thirties said to an older friend, "If I ever marry again, he better have money!"

Yes, money is a dominant element of our lives, but

we seldom talk about it in church. Oh, we talk about the need for more offerings, but we rarely discuss the meaning of money and its power. A cartoon in *The New Yorker* some time ago pictured two ministers standing in the pulpit, looking down on the communion table upon which the ushers had just placed the full and overflowing offering plates. One clergyman said to the other one, "It's pretty hard to keep from loving the stuff!"

Some Observations About Money

Money is a convenience we take for granted. We rarely analyze what it is. We just know we need more of it, and some of us will go to great lengths to satisfy that desire.

Sociologist Ruth Benedict did her research among the Zuni American Indian tribes of the Southwest. The Indian people, she says, love beads and jewelry. Many will give up their culture, customs, even their religion for wealth! Benedict says that all humans are prone to these tendencies. She summarizes by saying that, next to sex, the desire for money is the strongest drive within us.

Years ago I heard a clinical psychologist say that his clients spend 90 percent of their time thinking about money or the things it can provide. It's the desire for a better life, the pressure to keep up with the Joneses. And too much credit extended to support too high a lifestyle contributes to depression.

There never seems to be enough money if our value system is tuned to the search for more. Robert Heilbroner says, "Material advance has proved unable to satisfy the human spirit." In fact, Heilbroner continues, when we cross the threshold of basic comfort, the quality of life actually decreases with the increase of abundance and indulgence.

Nevertheless, we are a money-oriented society. If you ask a parent about a son or daughter living in another state, the parent likely will answer in terms of money. The parent may say, "Oh, Bob and Cindy are getting along just fine. They have good jobs, and they just bought a nice home." Rarely will the parent respond by saying something about the son or daughter's spiritual life.

Money is often explosive in the congregation. In July 1971 my wife and I moved to Indiana. Our district church conference was in session at the time on the campus of Goshen College. I dropped in at one of the sessions to see what issues Indiana-Michigan pastors and delegates were discussing. This was during the Vietnam War, and the government had legislated a telephone tax to help finance that conflict. There was an intensely heated debate over whether one ought to pay this tax.

Within some congregations questions about the amount of salary paid to the pastor can genuinely hinder fellowship. Or there may be divisions between the "haves" and the "have nots." Our pastors may preach against avarice, but in the next service encourage the members of their congregations to increase their tithes and offerings during the annual commitment period. In every case the increased offerings will come out of the members' accumulated income.

Money is a four-way paradox. (1) You can't live without it; (2) the Bible says the love of money is the root of all evil; (3) pastors preach against materialism; (4) yet the church keeps asking for more.

If money plays such a dominant role in our lives, we need to elevate it to a legitimate and responsible place on the congregation's agenda. We should analyze its meaning and establish a process for nonthreatening counsel for our members. Talking about money and teaching what the Bible says about it should be a regular practice for our congregations.

The Meaning of Money

Money as we know it came into existence about 700 B.C.E.[1] Before that, persons bartered everything. Three developments influenced the subsequent centuries:

First, radical individualism led to a money economy. Profits became a primary goal. Second, technology, an outgrowth of the money economy, led to machines which produced marketable goods. Third, credit was conceived as a way to gain greater leverage in producing goods.

Modern economics was launched when money became a medium of exchange. The barter system had not changed for thousands of years, but now everything took on new meaning. People became more manipulative, and more mobile. No doubt some of the problems of greed, selfishness, and the misuse of money had their roots in this period which historians have called the "radical individualism movement." The biblical prophets criticized this period.

Now let's take a closer look at money as a tool. We can describe it in four different ways.

First, *money is a medium of exchange,* a common denominator to which everything is reduced sooner or later. It is the medium to express value in a measura-

1. B.C.E. means *Before the Common Era.* C.E. means *Common Era.* The purpose of using this alternative to B.C. and A.D. is to avoid the parochial assumption inherent in B.C. (before Christ) and A.D. (*anno Domini* in the year of the Lord) that the whole world is Christian.

ble way. To say an automobile is worth seventy-two hogs is meaningless to most of us. Yet we all understand when we hear an automobile is worth $9,000. I heard a university professor declare that an idea is meaningless until it is translated into dollars and cents. What does it cost to put that idea or concept to work? Every service, every job, every piece of equipment, every employee benefit has a cost. All of the programs and services of an organization are reducible to the common denominator we call the budget—an instrument through which we express worth in a measurable way.

Second, *money is amoral*. Money is neither right nor wrong in and of itself. It takes on the morality of the spender. It becomes an influence for evil when our desire for more of it dominates our thinking. Such an attitude makes money a god in our lives—a deity with enormous power.

However, if we spend money as a social and religious expediter, it becomes a tool for good works, a special gift of God.

Third, *money in the hands of people is power and respect*. Men and women with wealth often exert power beyond the normal influence of other, less wealthy people. Look at the people who make up the hospital, college, university, or social service boards. Most are persons of wealth. In addition, persons in elected offices are often wealthy. Clearly, wealth is power and makes events and services happen.

Fourth, *money is a tool of creation*. We are born into a world of property, resources, and wealth. The Genesis story tells us to use that world to advance our purposes. As Christian people, our purpose is to continue the work Christ began, an impossible task if we don't use money in a responsible way.

The Bible cautions us that money can be dangerous. Fire is dangerous too, but no one argues that we should not use fire since it can get out of control. As Christians we need to walk beside each other in finding creative and effective uses for this tool of money! Quality Christian relationships with other members of our community of faith is probably more important in our decisions involving money than in any other area of our life. Our decisions of lifestyle, standards for living, children's education, use of leisure time, selection of friends, type of investments—nearly every decision we make has monetary implications.

The Biblical View of Money

The Bible does not speak of money in an abstract way. We know that Abraham, Jacob, Job, and Solomon were wealthy persons. In the Old Testament, wealth seems to be equated with God's favor. The story of Job and Malachi 3:10 suggest that if we are faithful, God will open the windows of blessings.

From Genesis to Malachi God's people are repeatedly shown that (1) God is owner through creation and redemption; (2) humans are stewards; (3) humanity responds by releasing gifts and services back to God; (4) faithfulness in handling material wealth and benevolences brings blessing and prosperity; and (5) unfaithfulness brings curse and tragedy.

The New Testament speaks about wealth in three ways: (1) as a source and supplier of our daily needs; (2) as a means of supporting the church; and (3) as an object of devotion—God vs. Mammon.

Jesus discusses wealth more than any other subject —more than love, peace, prayer, or forgiveness. He says repeatedly that our love for God and wealth can be in direct conflict with each other. Coming to terms with this conflict requires God's grace and love.

We know that Jesus had a treasurer—or at least a person who handled his money affairs. He frequently talked about money in a positive way. In fact, some Bible scholars say Jesus was an experienced businessperson through his father's construction company. They point out Jesus' many references to building and construction, travel, clothing, buying, selling, good dining, taxes, and more.

Perhaps the strongest, most positive of all of Jesus' teaching about money comes in Luke 16:1-15. It's a difficult passage for some pastors because they can't quite understand what Jesus is teaching. For this reason, many pastors avoid it. The passage appears in a series of discourses illustrating the true Israel and true service. It is the parable of the unjust steward. Here is the story.

A man of wealth left his affairs to the management of a steward. When the owner came back, he discovered the steward had not managed well. So he released him. The unhappy steward asked the question, "What shall I do now?" He was too old to do manual labor and didn't want to become a beggar on the street. Finally the idea came to him that he could make lifelong friends by falsifying records. He called two of the owner's debtors in and said to the first one, "How much do you owe?"

The debtor responded by saying he owed 100 barrels of oil (about $2,000). The manager told him to alter the records quickly and reduce the debt to 50 barrels.

The manager then asked the second debtor what he owed. That debt turned out to be 100 bushels of wheat (about $250). The manager told this debtor to alter the record and write down 80 bushels. When the owner discovered this dishonesty, he was quick to commend the manager for his shrewdness. "For the people of this world are more shrewd . . . than are the people of the light." The owner knew that the two debtors would reward the manager for years to come. Finally, in verse 9, Jesus says, "I tell you, use worldly wealth to gain friends for yourselves, so that when it is gone, you will be welcomed into eternal dwellings."

What is going on here? Is Jesus commending dishonesty? Or is he using satire to do some subtle and important teaching? Verse 8, freely translated, might read like this: "Look, the world knows what money is for. People of the world use money to gain their life's purposes and objectives. Now the children of light ought to be as smart as the children of darkness by using wealth to promote *their life's purposes and mission*—to continue the work Christ began."

If Christian people took Luke 16 seriously, it would revolutionize the church. The church would be able to strengthen many of its weaker programs—programs which are weak not because of poor leadership but because there are not enough funds available to do the work the leaders feel called to do.

Summary Biblical Statement on Money

There are many other Scriptures about money, but perhaps a summary statement will complete this brief overview.

(1) God owns everything. God operates as a chairperson of the board. Management decisions are up to us. However, we are guided by biblical guidelines.

(2) God gives us money to test our faithfulness and obedience. The rewards will come later. The parables

use the phrase, "enter into the joy of your Lord," to signal reward for obedience.

(3) It is not the possession of money but how we use it that determines faithfulness and obedience.

(4) Money has no creative function by itself. It never acts alone. Men and women foist their own values upon it when they use it for evil or for good.

(5) Money becomes an effective means of expressing concern for others when personal contact is not possible. We can help boat people from Vietnam, send hay to the drought-stricken farmers in the South, or offer a meal and a bed to the homeless—all through the long-distance power of our dollars.

(6) Jesus calls us to be faithful and obedient, not necessarily to be successful. The latter may be the result, but the Scriptures first demand obedience and faithfulness in our use of wealth.

Money in the Church's Program

Money is controversial, certainly, but it is also a tool given to us from the beginning to assist us in our Christian mission. It is incumbent upon the church to find ways to mobilize this gift so it becomes useful, as we have made fire a wonderful servant when it burns under control.

One way to think about money in the church is to adapt a concept I picked up at Columbia University in a class in Educational Finance. Let's begin with a triangle again, as we did in Chapter 4.

At the top of the triangle is our church's mission. I'll stay with the definition used in Chapter 2: "The Christian's mission is to continue the work Christ began." The statement is simple and easily understood—the New Testament reduced to a single sentence.

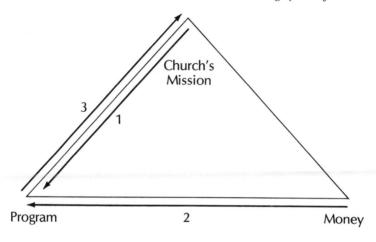

Program   2   Money

Diagram 4

Mission is central to our thinking, but meaningless until it is expressed in a program or activity. Here is where the human factor enters. In Genesis, the revelation begins in the creation story and comes to completion with the resurrection of Christ. Through our creation gifts of time, ability, and money, ours is the task to continue God's message through the generations—from person to person.

We continue the mission through various interactive programs. Believers gather into supportive networks we call churches. At the local level we establish individual congregations with teaching and outreach activities. Committees, sessions, and conferences meet at district, national, and international levels. We develop elaborate training programs and ways to call people "into mission." And through the generations, millions of persons have given themselves generously for a lifetime of service.

But too often the church has separated what God intended to be together. We have separated our time and ability gifts from the monetary gifts. We have preached Jesus' teachings on the potential evils of money but have not taught the positive idea that money makes possible programs that put into action our mission and beliefs. Notice the flow and direction of the arrows in the triangle. From mission, arrow one flows down into program. From money, arrow two flows back to program. If the program is conceived well, and people and money service that program, then arrow three flows back up to mission, putting that "reason for being" into action. I've heard it said this way: "Money puts feet under our mission!"

Money is essential for the vital program of the church, yet we have separated what God intended to be together—the program and the money essential for its implementation.

At Columbia University our professor drilled into us the importance of taxation, fees, and contributions for the educational efforts of the nation. His teachings are as true when applied to the church. We need to look at the opportunities before us to see how we can strengthen the church's mission through money. Money spent without a clear sense of mission is hopeless, but mission without money is helpless! I know from my own experience that there is a close relationship between an excellent program and the adequacy of dollars to put the program into action.

The Harry Emerson Fosdick quote at the beginning of this chapter is a marvelous statement. Through my money, I *can* speak languages unknown to me, lift burdens in many parts of the world, and be a part of saving lives wherever my fellow Christians are at work.

Because of the offering I place in the plate this

Sunday I am helping to place bread on the pastor's table and making it possible for him to do many pastoral duties. I am helping our youth to grow into responsible adults through the Youth Fellowship Program. I am at work in our church colleges, in missions around the world. I am helping to train pastors and other congregational leaders at our seminary. Through our Mennonite Central Committee I am distributing clothing and food to third-world families, working at national and international justice issues, even participating in some disaster relief in the United States. It's a thrill to know that through our money we can work in so many places. We are at work in mission around the world!

Time, ability, and money. These gifts must remain in balance. Obviously money will not do all the work. Likewise, the commitment of time and personal services alone is helpless. The call to obedience through coordinated effort is beautifully stated by Doris Longacre in her book, *Living More with Less.*[2]

> This book is for people who know something is wrong
> . . . and are ready to talk about change. This is a book
> about rediscovering what is good and true. . . . [Too
> often] we fail to fortify each other in our solid communities. . . . There is hope for us but no easy healing.
> There is truth but never without search. . . . When we
> come home from discussions, one voice still speaks in
> silence. For Christians it is the call to obedience.
> Without . . . that voice, and [our] answering again and
> again, there is no way to live.

In the chapters that follow, we look at ways to express our faithfulness in mission through our money.

---

2. Herald Press, Scottdale, Pa., 1980, pages 15-16.

6

God's Two-Step Plan to Finance the Church

Step 1: 1 Corinthians 16:1-4
2 Corinthians 8:1-14; 9:1-15

Step 2: Leviticus 25:1-55
Luke 4:16-19
Hebrews 11:1-16

GOD IS orderly and systematic in his approach to us. In creation he used six days to get our world in place and to establish man and woman. He continued his orderliness as he revealed himself through Abraham, Jacob, Joseph, David, and the prophets. In the fullness of time Jesus came, the disciples, the apostle Paul, and the early church. And now we as believers are in that tradition of orderliness!

Money is a constant reality in the lives of God's people. In 1 Chronicles 29 we read about Solomon's temple. Extravagant, yes! By some estimates, a temple like this would cost $50 million in 1990. The Bible shares stories of wealthy men—Job, Abraham, David, Solomon, Boaz. Paul speaks about the need for money to finance Christ's mission and in Romans 15 writes that he is on his way to Spain to establish the church. "I hope . . . to have you assist me on my journey there

[Spain], after I have enjoyed your company for a while" (v. 24). Isn't this an interesting way to ask for funding?

In 1 Timothy Paul speaks about the importance of adequate support for the elders (bishops). In Chapter 5 he says the elders who "rule well" are worthy of double salary, especially those who do preaching and teaching. Likewise, the Christian worker always deserves wages (vv. 17-18). When have you heard instruction like this in the church?

These Scripture references illustrate that God is straightforward about the importance of money in the church. There is no evidence that God intended the church to be poor or under-financed. There were poor people and abuses of wealth, but this was because of unfaithfulness and misuses of wealth by individuals or the social structures.

As God was orderly in the creation story, so God is orderly in the plan to finance the church. In this chapter we look at his two-step plan to do just that. Step 1 is *firstfruits*. Step 2 is *Jubilee*.

Some people understand firstfruits teaching. Nearly everyone has heard about it. Few practice it. But Jubilee is practically unknown in the church. People often associate *Jubilee* with a party rather than with a plan to provide major funding for the kingdom of God. Let's look at both plans in more detail.

Step 1: Firstfruits—Old Testament Views

One of the basic teaching methods of the Bible involves value-oriented stories. There are some commandments—especially in the Old Testament—and some illustrations and suggestions by which we are to model our lives. There are frequent stories of people gathering for worship. These worship experiences are regularly accompanied by a monetary gift—a symbolic representation of the worshipers giving themselves to a belief, a commitment, or a cause.

The first worship experience recorded in the Bible is in Genesis 4:3-4. Cain brought an offering from his crops and Abel offered the "firstborn of his flock." We are not told what prompted this act. The Bible just says, "In the course of time Cain. . . ." Apparently there is an instinctive need within us to recognize, worship, or honor God. The need was evident in Cain and Abel.

The next worship experience recorded comes after the Flood, when Noah built an altar and offered some clean animals and birds as a burnt offering to the Lord (Gen. 8:20-22).

The first mention of a measured offering of a tenth comes in Genesis 14:13-24, when Abram returns from a war and meets the high priest Melchizedek. Abram gives him "a tenth of everything" (v. 20).

The second mention of an offering of a tenth comes in Genesis 28, when Jacob has a dream of a struggle with God. Jacob makes a covenant with God that if he blesses him, he (Jacob) will give God a tenth of all future earnings (v. 22).

A fascinating story is told in Exodus 10, when Moses negotiates with Pharaoh to leave Egypt. Pharaoh tells Moses to go with his people, but to leave the flocks and herds. Moses responds by saying, "You must allow us to have sacrifices and burnt offerings. . . . Our livestock too must go with us. . . . We have to use some of them in worshiping the Lord our God" (vv. 25-26). You see, Moses did not know how to complete the act of worship unless he was able to give of his financial resources (flocks and cattle).

In Exodus 13 the Lord said "Consecrate to me every firstborn male . . . whether man or animal" (vv. 1-2). This is the first mention of firstfruits since Genesis 4. In verse 11 through verse 16 we have the beginning of the laws of firstfruits and the redemption of the first-born. This law of Moses continued to the time of Christ's eighth-day purification in Luke 2:21-24.

Exodus 23 and 34–36 contain great detail on how one should give. In Leviticus 27 we read the law concerning the tithe. The details seem repressive and unmotivating to us today. It's difficult to coordinate all the instructions on firstfruits and tithing, but apparently three tithes were requested.

The first tithe was collected annually for the priests. The second tithe was collected in years 1, 2, 4, and 5. It was known as the festival tithe. The third tithe was collected in years 3 and 6 for the poor, widows, and orphans.

During the seventh year the land was to lie fallow. That year was called Sabbath rest. However, some of the three tithes covered government *functions*—what we pay with our annual taxes. Frequent passages in Numbers and Deuteronomy show that tithing reminded the Israelites of what God did for them through history and kept them aware that God gave them wealth.

In Deuteronomy 26 we find many details on preparing the firstfruits for worship. Verses 16-19 contain a marvelous statement on the tithe as the expression of one's commitment and belief. Would to God that Christians today would equate their giving with their commitment!

> The Lord your God commands you this day to follow these decrees and laws [tithes and offerings]; carefully

observe them with all your heart and with all your
soul. You have declared this day that the Lord is your
God and that you will walk in his ways, that you will
keep his decrees, commands and laws, and that you
will obey him. And the Lord has declared this day that
you are his people, his treasured possession as he
promised, and that you are to keep all his commands.
He has declared that he will set you in praise, fame
and honor high above all the nations he has made and
that you will be a people holy to the Lord your God,
as he promised.   (Deut. 26:16-19)

Nehemiah tells the story of Israel rebuilding after
the captivity period. Against almost insurmountable
odds the Israelites forged ahead. "The people worked
with all their heart" (Neh. 4:6). Here was a rededication of faithfulness and obedience to God. They wor-
shiped at a new altar and symbolically gave of themselves by saying,

We also assume responsibility for bringing to the
house of the Lord each year the firstfruits of our crops
and of every fruit tree . . . [and] the firstborn . . . of
our herds and of our flocks . . . the first of our ground
meal, of our grain offerings. . . . And we will bring a
tithe of our crops to the Levites, for it is the Levites
who collect the tithes in all the towns where we work.
. . . We will not neglect the house of our God.
                                          (Neh. 10:35-39)

In Proverbs 3:9, tithe teaching is reinforced when
the writer says, "Honor the Lord with your wealth,
with the firstfruits of all your crops." In Malachi 3:10
we read, " 'Bring the whole tithe into the storehouse,
that there may be food in my house. Test me in this,'
says the Lord Almighty, 'and see if I will not throw
open the floodgates of heaven and pour out so much

blessing that you will not have room enough for it.' "

From Genesis to Malachi the record and the teachings on firstfruits and the tithe are consistent. To summarize is difficult, but perhaps we can list five summary statements on the firstfruits teaching in the Old Testament—the key ideas God wanted his people to know and practice.

(1) God is owner through creation and redemption.
(2) Men and women are stewards (*oikonomoi*).
(3) We are to return a portion of our wealth to God.
(4) Men and women are responsible to God (the owner) and to society for the management (*oikonomia*) of this trust.
(5) Faithfulness in this stewardship will bring blessing and prosperity. Unfaithfulness will bring curse and tragedy.

Point five is a legitimate deduction from the Old Testament. However, tithing for the sake of prospering materially puts the teaching on the wrong basis and defeats the basic motivation of gratefulness so clear in the New Testament. To ask someone to give with the promise of later material rewards defeats the spirit and purpose of stewardship as taught in Chapters 2 and 3 of this book. Rewards are sure, but they may not always be of a material nature.

New Testament Views on Firstfruits

It's interesting to observe that Jesus mentions the tithe only twice (Luke 11:42 and Luke 18:12). Paul never mentions the word. Both citations by Jesus are somewhat negative. In Luke 11 he says to the Pharisees, "You give God a tenth of your mint, rue, and all other kinds of garden herbs, but you neglect justice and the love of God. You should have practiced the latter without leaving the former undone." In Luke 18 Jesus quotes a Pharisee:

> 'I fast twice a week and give a tenth of all I get.' But the tax collector stood at a distance. He would not even look up to heaven, but beat his breast and said, 'God, have mercy on me, a sinner.' I tell you that this man, rather than the other, went home justified before God.

This is not to say Jesus did not believe in the tithe or firstfruits. But he did seem to place more emphasis on the spirit of the tithe than on its legal observance. He was deeply concerned about justice, peace, poor people, and widows. And he taught that money is one of the tools Christians use to address these issues.

While Paul does not mention the word *tithe*, he certainly discusses the spiritual symbolism of firstfruits and the need for generous giving. In 1 Corinthians 15, he speaks eloquently about the importance of the resurrection, referring to Jesus as a form of God's "firstfruits." In the following chapter, he treats giving more directly, saying that on the first day of the week we are to give as we prosper (vv. 1-4). Certainly Paul is not implying a lesser standard than in the Old Testament. I believe Paul thought his comments here were enough to motivate the Corinthian church.

However, the Corinthians did not respond. So one year later Paul wrote again in 2 Corinthians—not just four verses this time, but two whole chapters (2 Corinthians 8 and 9). He recites here some of the more pointed reasons in the New Testament for giving generously.

In each of Paul's epistles he asked for funds. He compared the generous giving of one congregation, the Philippians, to the more stingy responses of the people from Corinth. He seemed to know something about competition and motivational psychology!

Our summary of the New Testament teaching on firstfruits is shorter than the one from the Old Testament. Perhaps we can make two statements—one from the teachings of Jesus and one from the teachings of Paul.

First, nowhere in the Gospels does Jesus hold forth a lower standard than that established in the Old Testament. On the tithe, he simply says we should not legalistically perform the tithe and neglect the other important teachings, but instead seek a balance.

Second, Paul's teaching on firstfruits is spiritualized when he observes that Christians become a form of firstfruits to God through their redemption. To symbolize that position, Christians are to honor God on the first day of the week through generous giving. The amount is to be in keeping with their perception of how God prospers them. Paul urges that the giving be regular, systematic, and generous. His exact words leave nothing to the imagination: "See that you also excel in this grace of giving" (2 Cor. 8:7).

A Contemporary Application of the Firstfruits Principle

The firstfruits principle comes out of an agricultural economy. Crops, livestock, flocks, wool, skins, and wine were the media of exchange—all useful in their day. We need to adapt our firstfruit responses to fit our cash economy. How does the following modernized adaptation on firstfruits sound to you?

In a cash economy, Christians express a "firstfruits" response through an annual pledge or through a percentage of current and anticipated earnings over the following twelve months. The donors should determine the amount or percentage, but two standards should guide them—one from the Old Testament and one from the New. The Old Testament teaches the tithe and offerings (10 percent or more). The New Testament teaches the following process. (See 2 Cor. 8:5-15 and 2 Cor. 9:1-15.)

(1) "They gave themselves first to the Lord" (v. 5). Giving begins with dedication.

(2) "See that you also excel in this grace of giving" (v. 7). Generosity is the standard to follow.

(3) "Test the sincerity of your love" (v. 8). Generous giving is a sign of dedication and sincerity.

(4) "The gift is acceptable according to what one has, not according to what he does not have" (v. 12). Give as the Lord prospers you. A person cannot give what he does not have.

(5) "Then there will be equality" (v. 14). Approve a fair plan of distribution of the gifts to the various programs and agencies of the church.

(6) "Whoever sows sparingly will also reap sparingly, and whoever sows generously will also reap generously" (2 Cor 9:6). The law of the harvest applies to giving also.

(7) "Each man should give what he has decided in his heart to give . . . for God loves a cheerful giver" (v. 7). Giving must be voluntary, not coerced.

(8) "I am sending the brothers in order that . . . you may be ready [to give], as I said you would be" (2 Cor. 9:3). Sometimes a personal confrontation from a fellow believer motivates a generous response.

(9) "You will always be rich enough to be generous"

(2 Cor. 9:11, NEB). The joy of giving carries a blessing from God.

While the New Testament does not recommend an exact percentage as the Old Testament does, nothing leads us to believe the standards of giving are lower than in the Old Testament. Second Corinthians 9:11 indicates that a more generous response is normal.

With this contemporary adaptation of firstfruits, I can give anytime throughout the year toward my giving goal of 10 percent or more of my earnings. Thus, all my giving becomes symbolic of the "first things" I committed at the beginning of the year. This is in contrast to the person who has no goal and gives only if there is something left over at the end of the year. Call it *lastfruits* giving!

According to the nine-point plan above, a person does not need to give the same each month. When one receives income, one's firstfruits commitment is already in place. This allows a person with seasonal income to give the same way.

Now there are always some who oppose pledging because they don't know what the next year holds in store for them. "What if I become ill or I lose my job?" they ask. My response? If we are that uncertain about our future, why are we so ready to sign a four-year payment schedule for an automobile or a 30-year payment schedule on a home? Or what about our utility bills when we sign an occupancy service lease with the telephone or electric companies? Should all these payments have priority over our commitment to the kingdom of God?

Still others ask, On what part of my income do I figure my firstfruits—gross or net? Before taxes or after? Before my IRA payment or after? I advise that you figure your firstfruits giving on your "adjusted gross income," to borrow a tax term.

The above are only suggestions. You may have other views. Certainly the intent is to be faithful and obedient to God's word. If you have a question, discuss the issue with others you trust in your congregation.

Another frequent question is, How does one establish a year in advance a church budget or a congregational goal based on firstfruits giving from the membership? This is the toughest question of all! There is no one satisfactory solution. Here is a suggestion for your treasurer and finance committee. Begin by completing this form.

1. Number of households in your congregation:

_____

(An earning husband and an earning wife are one household. A single earning person is one household also.)

2. Estimated median income per household:
$_____
(Get this figure from the July (or August) issue of *Sales Marketing and Management*. See discussion below for more detail.)

3. Multiply line 2 by line 1: $_____
(This is the estimated adjusted gross income of all households in your congregation.)

4. Multiply line 3 by 10 percent $_____
(This is the estimated tithe of your congregation.)

5. Goal established by your congregation
$_____

The pastor can provide information for Line 1. Line 2 is controversial. Most people will not fill out forms reporting their adjusted gross income and to request it can create dissension. But pertinent information is available. Go to your public library and ask for the latest July (or August) issue of *Sales Marketing and Management* (SMM). There are two issues in July—one with the usual articles and the second with *Annual EBI Survey* printed on the cover. *EBI* is the abbreviation for Effective Buying Income. You should read the full description of EBI, but here is the interpretation.

First, the printed statistics are all taken from the individual 1040 Federal Tax Form filed by April 15 of the current year.

Second, the figures reported in SMM are median incomes (not average). The median income is the effective buying income after taxes, as filed by the individual of every state, county, county seat, or major metropolitan area in the United States or Canada.

This SMM median income amount is a different figure from the one I suggested earlier in this chapter to calculate the tithe. I said one should figure the tithe on one's adjusted gross income before taxes. I know of no other way to establish a congregation's adjusted gross median income. The SMM magazine figure is the next-best estimate, yet it is a compromise. If you want to add to this median SMM figure an estimated corrective amount for the income tax paid, that is okay. Next, find your state or province listed in SMM, then look for your county statistics. It lists income by median and for each quartile. You will have to decide which figure is most applicable to your congregation. Place the selected amount on line 2 above.

Lines 3 and 4 are routine.

Line 5 requires a judgment. Few people will do all

their giving through the congregation. Some hold back a portion of their tithe for special appeals made by worthy charitable organizations within the church or community. Also, some wealthy persons probably will not give as much through their congregations as they give on a direct basis. For instance, let's say a person of wealth gives $100,000 a year. Placing that amount into a typical congregational offering will intimidate the $25-a-week contributor. These persons of wealth are wonderful individuals for major fund drives within the whole framework of charitable projects.

Another way to calculate line 5 is to take your annual every-member commitment forms and add them together. For those households not filling out an every-member commitment card, your church treasurer or committee can work through lines 1 through 5 using the SMM magazine figures.

Firstfruits Conclusion

For some, the last several pages may seem impractical. However, all people need models to follow. The above five-step process is one model. If you have a better way to estimate your congregation's tithe potential, use it. The only standard God requires is faithfulness and obedience to the Word. To be faithful requires a satisfactory financial support. The NT standard is to give "as God has prospered " each one (1 Corinthians 16:2, KJV). Certainly this standard is equal to or higher than the OT teaching of a firstfruit share (tithe). Remember, there is a close relationship between the quality of a program and the financial support to undergird it.

I have found when people take ownership in a movement, a cause, or a vision, they respond by wanting to "live into" that vision. They volunteer their personal resources, including finances, just as parents work to help their children meet the opportunities at hand. Likewise, it is important that church leadership keeps alive the purposes and programs of the church. Then our families will respond voluntarily and the mechanics of the preceding pages serve as reinforcements, not prime motivators. When the vision is clear, the "Zacchaeus factor" spoken of in Chapter 3 motivates generous response.

The firstfruits teaching in this chapter is equally applicable to people of modest, average, or high income. Persons of all levels are called to meet the obedience test. Remember the story of the widow's mite. Her response was one of faithfulness as well as obedience.

The following page will be a fitting close to this section on firstfruits. It is a selection of Scriptures encouraging us to be obedient in our giving to the church. Feel free to reproduce the page and distribute it in your congregation when you are teaching firstfruits. It will be an effective reading as a devotional or as a closing meditation. Everyone should have a copy —both to hear the Word and to have the visual image of the big 1.

Selected Scripture Readings on Firstfruits[1]

"When you come into the land which the Lord your God is giving you . . . you shall take the firstfruits of all the produce of the soil . . . . You shall go to the place which the Lord your God will choose . . . for his Name and come to the priest. . . . You shall say to him, 'I declare this day to the Lord your God that I have entered the land which the Lord swore to our forefathers to give us.' . . . Then you shall solemnly recite before the Lord your God:

>'My father was a homeless Aramaean who went down to Egypt with a small company and lived there until they became a great, powerful, and numerous nation. But the Egyptians ill-treated us, humiliated us and imposed cruel slavery upon us. Then we cried to the Lord the God of our fathers for help, and he listened to us and saw our humiliation, our hardship and distress; and so the Lord brought us out of Egypt with a strong hand and outstretched arm, with terrifying deeds, and with signs and portents. He brought us to this place and gave us this land. . . . And now I have brought the firstfruits of the soil which thou, O Lord, hast given me.' You shall then set the basket before the Lord your God and bow down in worship before him. You shall all rejoice, you and the Levites and the aliens living among you, for all the good things which the Lord your God has given to you and to your family."

"Abel brought some of the first-born of his flock, the fat portions of them. The Lord received Abel and his gift with favour." "Honour the Lord with your wealth as the first charge on all your earnings." "Set your mind on God's kingdom and his justice before everything else, and all the rest will come to you as well. . . . On the first day of every week, each of you is to put something aside . . . as he may prosper. . . . I say this not as a command, but to prove . . . that your love also is genuine. . . . You will always be rich enough to be generous."

---

1. The Scriptures for this graphic are adapted from the New English Bible and the Revised Standard Version. The Scripture references and format were selected by John Mosemann. Reprinted by permission. The references are Deuteronomy 26:1-11; Genesis 4:4; Proverbs 3:9; Matthew 6:33; 1 Corinthians 16:2; 2 Corinthians 8:8; and 2 Corinthians 9:11a.

Step 2: Jubilee—Biblical Background

Now we move to step 2 of God's plan to finance the church. Step 1, firstfruits, grows out of current income. Step 2, Jubilee, grows out of a lifetime of accumulated savings, after (symbolically) 50 years of work and service.

Jubilee was given by the Lord to help deal with the social disorder among the tribes caused by slavery, enormous debt, landlessness, exploitation of the poor, and so on. These disorders placed heavy yokes and unequal burdens upon the people. Israelite justice called for protection of the weak.

Jubilee literally means celebration—in this case, a celebration at the end of life. It grew out of a system containing a series of sabbaths. For example, after each six days Israel was to observe a sabbath on the seventh day. After each six years the land was to lie fallow during the seventh. This was known as the sabbath rest year. After seven sabbath rest years (7 x 7 = 49, or on the 50th year), there was a Jubilee. This was the granddaddy of all sabbaths!

At the end of life (symbolically, after 50 years), the land leases all reverted back to the tribe, symbolizing that God was the land's true owner (Psalm 24:1). Various tribe members were entitled only to cropping rights. For a detailed description of what one could or could not do under the plan for the Jubilee, read Leviticus 25:1-55; 27:16-25; and Numbers 36:4..

On the 51st year, a tribe member could buy 50 years of cropping rights from the tribe. For instance, a family could farm a tract for 30 years, then resell the remaining 20 years to another tribe member. At the end of 50 years, all land came back for reselling to other willing tribe buyers. There were other restrictions too, but this is enough to let you know how the system worked.

Every 50 years (in the year of Jubilee) large sums of money came to the tribes as new cropping rights were sold for the next 50-year period. This money helped solve the social problems listed in paragraph two of this section, making it impossible for the rich to get richer and the poor to get poorer.

Elements of the Old Testament Jubilee plan are useful to us today as we grow to Christian maturity.

First, Jubilee limits uncontrollable greed and acquisition (Lev. 25:17-24; Luke 18:18-27; Matt. 6:19-34).

Second, Jubilee helps us identify with our neighbors, toward whom our love is evidence of our love for God (Lev. 25:35ff.; Matt. 22:34-40).

Third, Jubilee calls us to remember God's purpose for his people and to reorder life by that purpose. Deuteronomy 31:10-13 and Romans 12 gives a similar sequence: God's mercies, God's will, God's life in his people.

Fourth, Jubilee is a liberation into the highest concept of servanthood. We become disciples to the redeeming God! (Lev. 25:52-55; John 8:31-38).

Jesus' entire ministry addressed the Old Testament expressions of the Jubilee model of liberty. At the beginning of his ministry, he said, "The Spirit of the Lord is on me, because he has anointed me to preach good news to the poor. He has sent me to proclaim freedom for the prisoners and recovery of sight for the blind, to release the oppressed, to proclaim the year of the Lord's favor" (Luke 4:18-19).

Jesus spelled Jubilee in terms of loving God, loving neighbor, and loving self. Jubilee involved using accumulated resources at the end of one's life—the 50th working year—in lifting yokes, distributing financial resources, ending bondages, and releasing one's life for God. Jubilee made possible large sums of money for solving tribal problems and meeting responsibilities.

In spite of the elaborate and beautiful plan, Bible scholars say Jubilee didn't work. The people were neither obedient or faithful to God's plan to work at tribal social and financial needs.

But if it didn't work then, is that a reason we shouldn't teach it today? Why not try it? It may work! Most people have never heard of Jubilee because most ministers have never taught it. My experience with Jubilee has been positive. People like it and respond generously when they understand the principle.

A Contemporary Update on Jubilee

Is a contemporary application of Jubilee possible? Or is it an Old Testament principle without current significance? The answer to the first question is yes. To the second, no!

It is possible to practice the Year of Jubilee through our estate planning and our wills. Such a measure involves distributing our estates, either before or after death, in a more equitable manner within the global ministry of the church. Today, relatively few people include the church in their wills or estate planning.

Perhaps the contemporary counterparts to the tribes of the Old Testament are our present denominational structures. Why shouldn't we want to see our own denomination's voice as strong as possible in missions, education, relief administration, peace and justice issues, publishing, and mutual aid? Through our wills, large blocks of funds can be released for these opportunities.

Most people are like the people of the Old Testament. They don't do it! I might give a lifetime to singing songs such as "I Love Thy Kingdom, Lord" and "My Jesus, I Love Thee." I might talk long and hard in Sunday school about what the church ought to be doing. But when it comes to planning my estate, I leave little or nothing to the church! What kind of "Last Will and Testament" is that?

It is clear to those who read the financial reports of our church boards and agencies that few people include the church in their estate planning. *This should not be!* The legal structures are all in place to make estate planning easy to do. There are legal provisions for wills, many types of trusts and annuities, and ways to transfer stock—often at a tax saving to the giver. Too often people have missed their last opportunity to tell their family and posterity that the church is important to them. People should consider passing on opportunity to their children, but they should also pass substantial money and assets to the church to assist in its administration and programs.

Some Examples of Jubilee

During the 1920s a young man in Pennsylvania had marital problems. Devastated and finding himself in an unsympathetic community, he left the area, moving west to begin his life again. He stopped in Idaho, invested in farmland and mining stocks, and made some money. He found a church there and made a new start.

During the 1950s I began to call on him and suggested he set up a scholarship endowment fund. I suggested he begin the fund while he was living and complete the plan through his will at death. He agreed.

Years later I stopped to see him again. After the

usual small talk, he asked me to read aloud a letter from a missionary in Japan. His eyes were poor, he said, and it was difficult for him to read. The letter told of some exciting things happening in Japan. Then it closed by saying, "As you know, Brother Kulp, I was one of your first scholarship recipients. Without your scholarship help I would never have been able to go on to college and prepare for mission work. Thanks for your help. Sincerely yours, —."

I looked at Brother Kulp and saw that he was moved to tears. Wiping his eyes, he said to me, "I didn't know an 80-year-old person in a wheelchair could be so useful." Here was a person in Idaho very much at work in Japan. How? Through his money. Since that time he has gone to his reward and his estate has placed more money into the scholarship plan. Even though Brother Kulp is not here, he is still speaking and perpetuating those values to which he gave a lifetime. This is a modern-day expression of Jubilee!

My mother made her first will at about age 90. She became a widow at 42 and has had nothing but economic struggles all her life. She kept telling me she wanted a will. I said, "Mother, you don't need a will. There is little in your estate. You won't have a tax problem." Finally she said, "But I want to leave something to the church. I want people to know the church has been important to me!"

I nearly jumped out of my chair. Of course she should have a will! It's the only way she can leave money to the church. Her will is now complete, and she has designated $100 to each of two colleges, a mission board, and a retirement home—a total of $400. This estate gift is as big for my mother as the thousands of dollars Brother Kulp put into the scholarship plan. I doubt that my mother's estate will have $400 in it after funeral expenses, but you can be sure her family will make up the money in her name.

In Hebrews 11 we read about the great heroes of the faith: Abel, Enoch, Noah, Abraham, Isaac, Jacob, Sarah, Rahab. These all died but through their faith are still speaking.

Likewise, through our estate planning, we demonstrate the preeminence of Christ in our lives. If many people were to practice this concept of Jubilee, it would release millions of dollars to make the church even stronger in her witness around the world.

Summary

God does not intend the church to be without adequate resources to carry out God's mission. God has given us a two-step plan to finance the church: firstfruits and Jubilee. The effectiveness of God's plan depends upon our giving firstfruits of our current income throughout life and by supporting the church by practicing Jubilee at life's close.

7

Creative Vehicles to Use in Charitable Giving

Acts 11:27-29; Philippians 4:14-20
1 Timothy 6:17-19; Titus 3:13-14
Hebrews 13:15-16; 1 John 3:17-18
3 John 1:5-8

IN THIS CHAPTER I will discuss some of the creative vehicles Christians use to distribute their charitable gifts to the many agencies and causes they want to support. There are no specific references in the Bible on this issue. The only method of giving in the Scriptures is the outright gift of cash or the sharing of time and personal possessions.

To continue my practice of beginning each chapter with appropriate Scripture references, I have listed some infrequently cited passages. In these Paul either thanks members of the established church for their giving or asks for cash gifts to support his new efforts in church planting.

Paul makes it abundantly clear that generous giving is an effective way for Christians to express their support of New Testament evangelists and their church planting efforts. Through their giving, Christians could release Paul and associates to spend their whole time propagating the gospel. Paul was able to rent a house in Rome and make it the center of his efforts to evangelize the city. Gifts from the Philippians paid Paul's staff allowances and travel for Tychicus, Epaphroditus, Epaphras, Aquila, Priscilla, Onesimus, Demas, John Mark, Silas, Phoebe, Luke, Timothy, Titus, and, of course, Paul—a group of fourteen persons. This was quite a mission endeavor! *Money* put feet under the apostle Paul's mission program.

Some New Ways of Giving Now

People are surprised to discover there are many new ways of giving that can strengthen the church and other worthy charitable causes. At the same time, these ways can: (1) increase the giver's own personal income; (2) facilitate estate planning; (3) reduce current income taxes and future estate taxes; and (4) benefit heirs.

It is my hope that this "how to" chapter will serve as an idea starter and begin a new era for some readers. Those who wish to make a larger gift should gather a team of persons to work with them. This team might include an accountant, a trust officer or other financial planner, an attorney, and people from the agencies the person wants to assist. Counselors from the denominational foundation office can be quite helpful. Mennonites depend on the Mennonite Foundation (Goshen, Indiana, and Winnipeg, Manitoba). Members of other denominations can talk with their pastor to find the address of their own foundation. All of these officers are ready to spend the time it takes to design a plan tailored to each unique situation.

As you read through the various plans you will see that some of them require individual calculations based on age. With these calculations in hand you will find a new opportunity to become a partner in the many Christian service agencies continuing Christ's work. Persons sixty years or older can approach these thirteen ways as an opportunity to practice the biblical concept of Jubilee.

Appreciated Assets Make Good Gifts

Many people think charitable contributions involve only cash gifts from their current incomes. However, almost anything of value can be contributed to a charity. Here is an expanded list of assets that appreciate with time and make appropriate gifts for most charities.

1. Stocks
   a. publicly traded stock
   b. closely held stock
2. Bonds
3. Other Securities
   a. Certificates of Deposit
   b. Treasury Bills
   c. Mutual Funds
4. Real estate
   Transfer of full ownership or an undivided interest of:
   (1) Homes
   (2) Land
5. Life Insurance
   a. Existing policies
   b. New policies
6. Personal Property
   a. antiques
   b. works of art

 c. jewelry
 d. cars, trucks, mobile homes, RVs
 e. livestock and poultry
 f. farm products or equipment
 g. any collection of value
7. Individual Retirement Accounts (must recognize accumulated assets as taxable income before transfer is made)
8. Other
 a. notes and leases
 b. mortgages
 c. land contracts
 d. business inventories
 e. royalties

The present United States income tax laws require persons to report all noncash gifts (except publicly traded securities) over $500 to the Internal Revenue Service on Form 8283, filed with their income tax return. If the property is valued over $5,000, a certified appraisal must be attached to Form 8283. Your CPA or tax consultant can help you with this procedure.

Some Added Considerations

Making a contribution is a personal and meaningful way to support a charitable agency. The apostle Paul recognized this in his day and shared with donors what they accomplished through their gifts to the church.

To make a gift even more personal, you may want to consider establishing a memorial or tribute gift in honor of a family member. An endowment, a building, a scholarship, lectureship, a piece of equipment—almost anything can be an appropriate memorial or tribute designation for your gift.

Some persons are shy about having their own names appear with a significant gift. We have been taught such publicity is a wrong display of pride. But isn't it interesting that authors of books and articles and researchers of new discoveries do not resist being named? If money is equal to time and ability, why shouldn't we appropriately recognize a gift of money as we do the gift of a magazine article, a book, or a discovery? Can you imagine a book written without the author's name attached?

Thirteen Gift Plans[1]

Now we will look at some specific vehicles for making gifts to advance the kingdom of God. Each plan will follow a similar descriptive outline so they can be compared. Your accountant or another financial counselor can answer your questions about which plan or combination of plans suits your situation. The development officer from the charity you're interested in can be helpful too.

Plan 1—Outright Gift

Brief description. The outright gift undergirds all philanthropy and is the most familiar method of giving. It consists of an asset given irrevocably to a charity. Individuals who are in a position to make this

---

1. The thirteen plans listed here are adapted from a publication prepared by the Mennonite Foundation and Goshen College. Each plan is described in a generic sense and can be useful for any charity in the United States having a 501(c)3 status. This status applies to all church agencies and most charitable organizations. Reprinted with permission. Comparable information for Canada may be obtained from Mennonite Foundation of Canada. See Appendix B for *Mennonite Resource Persons* and addresses.

kind of gift are those with capital assets or income they do not need for their own financial security.

Type of gift acceptable.
1. Cash
2. Property: residence, farm, ranch, resort property, community property
3. Stocks, bonds, or other marketable assets
4. Personal property
5. Insurance policies
6. Individual retirement accounts (IRAs)

Income tax deduction.
1. Cash: 50%
2. Property, stocks, bonds held long-term: 30% (of adjusted gross income)
3. Gifts for the use of charity (lead trusts)
   - funded with appreciated property: 20%
   - funded with cash: 30%

Carry forward rule: Donors who reach their deduction limit in the first year can carry forward the excess for five years (for a total of six years). Outright gifts, real estate, and stock held long-term are deductible at current value.

Capital gain implication. Taxes on capital gains are avoided. However, the alternative minimum tax may apply if the gift property is highly appreciated and the donor has a high income. Property is receipted at current appraised value. Highly appreciated low-yield assets such as stocks are especially attractive as a gift.

Recommended for. This plan is for donors who want the church or charity to benefit immediately from a gift. Also, it is for donors who can use immediate maximum tax benefits.

Plan 2—Income Stream

Brief description. This plan allows you to provide for both heirs and the church or charity with a single bequest. Because it multiplies the value of the bequest, this plan has advantages for both the donor and the beneficiaries. Moreover, the donor distributes his or her estate over time, the way he or she accumulated it.

Suppose you want to leave your estate or a sum of money to your children or other relatives or friends, but you also want to support a specific charity. These interests can be combined in an income stream. You trickle out income from the bequest to your heirs over a period of years, after which the principal goes to the charity.

For example, suppose your will provides that property valued at $100,000 goes into a charitable unitrust at your death with these provisions. (1) Six percent of the trust value will be paid annually to your children and divided among them. (2) Payments to the children will continue for 15 years. Then the trust assets will be transferred to the charity for a specific purpose. During the 15 years, your children receive at least $90,000 and the charity will still receive at least $100,000.

Acceptable gifts. All or a portion of estate assets.

Implementation. The vehicle used is a charitable testamentary trust (a trust provided for in your will and implemented at your death). Your beneficiaries receive a predetermined percentage annually for a specified number of years after which the principal is transferred to the charity and the trust dissolved.

Rate of income to heirs. If you disburse 7 percent annually to your heirs, they will receive an amount equal to the original bequest in 14.3 years. Six percent requires 16.7 years and 8 percent 12.5 years.

Charitable benefit. When the time for the trust expires, the principal is turned over to the charity for use as the donor specifies.

Recommended for. This plan is for persons who want to spread out the inheritance rather than give heirs access to a lump sum and who also want to make a generous gift to a charitable cause.

Plan 3—Gift with Retained Life Estate

Brief description. In this plan you are entitled to an income tax deduction for a gift of a remainder interest in real property if the remainder interest is in a personal residence or farm. You can enjoy your home or farm for the rest of your life and still know that some day it will be used for a purpose you designate.

Acceptable gifts.

1. *Personal residence.* Any property used by a donor as his or her personal residence, even if it is not a principal residence, is acceptable.

2. *A farm.* Any land used by a donor or his or her tenant for the production of crops, fruits, other agricultural products, or for feeding livestock is acceptable.

Gift value determination. To determine the tax deduction for the gift of a home or farm, the following information is needed: the fair market value; the estimated nondepreciable value of the residence; the estimated age of the residence; and the estimated useful life of the residence.

Sale of gift with retained life estate. If, after a period of years, the donor and the charity agree to sell their interests to a third party, such a sale can be negotiated. The share received by each is dependent on the donor's age and life expectancy at the time of the sale.

Current tax benefits. The gift entitles the donor to a charitable tax deduction in the year of the gift. The size of the deduction is based on the age of the individual donor(s) at the time of the gift with a five-year carry forward provision (a total of six years).

Farm management and residence maintenance. The donor is responsible for all management, maintenance, and taxes. The donor also retains all the income. At the donor's death, the farm or residence is used for the purposes of the charity as designated by the donor.

Recommended for. This plan is for donors interested in receiving immediate income tax benefits while they continue living in their home. Because a donor has given his or her property while living, there are no estate taxes on the property when the estate is settled. Therefore, the Federal Estate Tax may be computed at much lower rates. At the same time, the charity has received a gift that is the fair market value of the property, not that value minus estate taxes.

Plan 4—Life Insurance as a Gift

Brief description. Most life insurance is bought with one thought in mind: to provide your family with financial security should you die. As you grow older, the purposes of life insurance are often met by other means and the insurance policy makes a fine charitable gift. Specific tax benefits are available if you assign life insurance to a charity as a gift.

Tax treatment. A donor irrevocably assigns his or her whole life insurance policy to a charity. This plan has substantial tax benefits. If premiums remain to be paid, the tax deduction is slightly above cash surrender value. If paid up, the deduction is generally the policy replacement cost. In addition, because the policy is assigned irrevocably to the charity, the value of your estate does not include the face value of the policy, which may result in federal estate tax savings.

There is a third tax advantage. When you pay the premium each year, you can treat your payment as a charitable contribution. It is deductible from your federal income tax.

A variation. Some donors purchase a policy on their lives and immediately make the charity the owner and beneficiary. In this case the annual premium becomes a tax deductible gift. After a number of years the dividends and paid-up additions provide the annual premium payment. The popular name of this policy is "vanishing premium." Your insurance agent will advise on the technical steps. Here are two illustrations:

Age		Annual premium (tax deductible) for 5 years. Face Amount		Age		Single premium (tax deductible) Face Amount	
		$30,000	$60,000			$50,000	$100,000
30	M	$341	$554	45	M	$4,552	$7,593
	F	283	424		F	3,096	5,862
40	M	507	902	55	M	7,965	15,524
	F	409	702		F	5,863	11,322
				65	M	16,107	31,753
					F	11,656	22,855

Recommended for. This plan is for donors who no longer need insurance protection and can use their insurance policies for tax benefits now. Or donors who want to make a major gift to a charity in the future and assure it through a life policy that makes the charity the owner and beneficiary. This plan is an excellent way to make a major gift on an installment plan basis.

Plan 5—Farm to Family: Assets to the Charity

Brief description. Many charities have constituent donors who are owners of family farms. They have an interest in passing on the opportunity to sons or daughters, but they want the charity ultimately to receive a major gift. If they sell the farm, they may pay major capital gains taxes. In Plan 5 the farm (or portion) is transferred to the charity. After the gift is completed, the charity may agree to rent and ultimately sell the farm back to the sons or daughters.

How it's done. The donor makes an outright gift of the farm (or portion) to the charity. This gift entitles the donor to a charitable contribution of up to 30 percent of the donor's adjusted gross income with a five-year carryover for any excess. Further, the donor avoids income taxes on capital gains and likely avoids most estate taxes. The alternative minimum tax may apply if the gift property is highly appreciated and the donor has a high income.

The charity agrees to rent the farm to the son or daughter for cash. The charity, as owner, pays the taxes. At some point the charity may sell the farm to the son or daughter at the fair market value. In this plan the farm is kept in the family. The charity uses the money for endowment in its continuing programs. (The donor can specify how the charity is to use the endowment. *A note of caution* to the donor: Rent and sale terms cannot be prearranged but must be negotiated after the land is received by the charity.)

Charted, the plan looks like this.

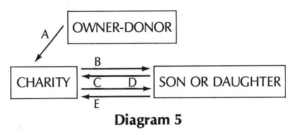

Diagram 5

- The owner-donor transfers the farm (or portion of it) to the charity.
- The charity rents the farm to a son or daughter.
- The son or daughter pays rent to the charity.
- At some point the charity may sell the land to the son or daughter at the current fair-market value.
- The son or daughter pays installment payments or cash to the charity for use in the endowment program or other purpose designated by the donor.

Recommended for. This plan is for donors who are charitably minded but who do not have cash to give; all of their assets are tied up in land. This is a way to preserve the family farm for the family and pass on the assets to the church or charity. It is a form of the biblical concept of Jubilee!

Plan 6—Revocable Charitable Remainder Trust

Brief description. Cash or property is revocably transferred by the donor to a foundation, which acts as a trustee for the benefit of the charity and the donor. (The donor can ask for it back if it's needed in the future.) The foundation invests and reinvests the assets in a separate fund. The beneficiary receives annually an amount equal to the actual income earned.

Acceptable gifts. Cash or marketable securities.

Suggested amount. $10,000 or more.

Beneficiary provision. It can be for more than two lives.

Rate of income. The annual income paid to the beneficiary is equal to the distributable income earned in the revocable trust.

Current tax benefits. First, the amount paid to the income beneficiary retains the character it had in the trust and is taxed the same. Examples are ordinary income, capital gains income, tax free income, and other income. Second, since the gift is revocable, the donor receives no charitable contribution deduction.

Capital gain implications. If the gift transferred is long-term appreciated property, and it is sold by the trustee, the capital gain generated is recognized by the donor in the year of the sale.

Estate tax implications. A one-life revocable trust for the donor's life is completely excluded from his or her estate.

In a two-life revocable trust, if the second life is the donor's spouse, the spouse's interest is not included in the donor's taxable assets. However, if the second beneficiary is someone other than a spouse and survives the donor-beneficiary, the value of the survivor's right to the trust fund is subject to tax in the donor's estate.

Gift tax implications. If the donor is the income beneficiary, there is no gift tax on the revocable trust. If an individual other than the donor is the income beneficiary, the donor is subject to gift tax.

Reporting to donor. First, at the time of the gift, the charity and the foundation provide the donor a revocable charitable remainder trust agreement. Second, the foundation provides the income beneficiary Schedule K-1 (Form 1041) and a complete annual financial statement of the fund. Schedule K-1 (Form 1041) reports the total income payments made in the taxable year just ended.

Recommended for. This plan is for donors who have limited assets and believe they may need the principal returned to them in case of lingering illness or other unforeseen need. If the trust is never revoked, all the assets belong to the charity to be used as the donor directs. The donor's estate may have reduced probate and administrative costs.

Plan 7—Charitable Bailout (for owners of closely held family corporations)

Brief description. The IRS Code is direct and to the point. Sometimes through a circuitous route it is possible to use the code to achieve family goals that lead to significant tax savings. One such route approved by IRS is called the *charitable bailout.*

Here the donor is the majority or sole owner of a closely held corporation. He or she is charitably motivated but wants any gift to come from the corporation's earnings. The donor knows a personal gift is more advantageous than a corporate gift. The corporate gift is limited to 10 percent of its taxable income. Further, a corporate gift does not help the donor's personal gift deductions. There is an alternative whereby the individual gives personally owned corporate stock.

How it's done. A charitable bailout works this way. The donor makes an outright gift to charity of shares of stock in his or her corporation. The gift entitles him or her to a charitable contribution deduction. After the gift the charity and the corporation agree to a redemption of these shares. The corporation gets back its stock, and the charity receives cash or an installment contract. In legal circles this plan is referred to as the *Palmer case.*

Charted, the plan looks like this.

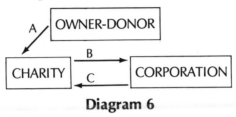

Diagram 6

- The owner-donor transfers shares to the charity.

- Sometime later the corporation redeems the shares from the charity.

- The corporation now has the stock and pays the charity the current fair market value.

IRS position. Following the Palmer case, IRS agreed to the plan in Revenue Ruling 78-197. The court found that the gift was valid and gave the charity full dominion and control over the shares. Although the redemption was anticipated, the charity was not a sham and had no enforceable legal obligation to sell the stock to the corporation. Therefore, the taxpayer realized no income from the sale.

What to do. For many years, the charitable bailout has been an attractive way for owners of closely held corporations to withdraw earnings tax-free from their businesses. With IRS's acquiescence in *Palmer*, this strategy becomes even more appealing. However, before any charitable bailout is attempted, a taxpayer should bear in mind the following requirements.

- The charity must not be a "sham."

- The transfer of stock must be a valid gift.

- If the corporation expects to liquidate, the gift of the stock must be made prior to the adoption of a plan of liquidation.

• The charity must be under no legal obligation to sell its shares.

• The corporation must not have the right to compel the charity to sell its shares.

Recommended for. This plan is for owners of closely held family corporations who are charitably motivated and want to find ways to retain the corporation in the family.

Plan 8—Charitable Gift Annuity

Brief description. Cash or marketable securities or both are irrevocably transferred to the charity for the promise to pay a fixed amount annually to the donor for life.

Acceptable gifts. Cash or marketable securities.

Suggested amount. Any amount of $1,000 or more.

Beneficiary provision. Only two beneficiaries can be named, usually the donor and spouse, but it can be the donor and someone else.

Rate of payments. The annual rate of return depends on the age of the beneficiary(ies) at the time of the gift and remains constant for life. Personnel at the donor's charity have the latest rates.

Current tax benefits. A substantial part of the annual annuity payment the donor receives is tax-free for his or her calculated life expectancy after which the entire annuity payment becomes taxable. The percentage is determined by the age of the income beneficiary(ies). Personnel at the donor's charity can calculate the tax-free portion when the ages of the beneficiary(ies) are known. *This tax-free feature gives an unusually high effective return.* The following table provides actual gift annuity rates for a person at different ages in a 28 percent income-tax bracket:

Person's Age	Actual Payment Rate	Effective Taxable Yield
60	7.0%	8.0%
65	7.3%	8.4%
70	7.8%	9.1%
75	8.5%	10.0%
80	9.6%	11.4%
85	11.4%	13.6%
90	14.0%	16.8%

• The gift entitles the donor to a charitable tax deduction in the year of the gift. The size of the deduction is based on the age of the income beneficiary(ies) at the time of the gift.

• If the gift annuity is funded with cash, the ceiling on the deduction is 50 percent of the donor's adjusted gross income with a five-year carryover for any excess.

• If the gift annuity is funded with long-term appreciated property, the ceiling on the deduction is 30 percent of the donor's adjusted gross income with a five-year carryover for any excess.

Capital gains implication. For a gift of appreciated property held long-term, the capital gain on only the investment portion of the gift annuity is reported and spread over the donor's life expectancy. The alternative minimum tax may apply.

Estate tax implications. A one-life gift annuity is excluded from the donor's estate, thereby possibly reducing federal estate taxes. In a two-life gift annuity, if the second annuitant is the spouse of the donor, the spouse's interest is not included in the donor's taxable estate if the executor makes a Qualified Terminable Interest Property (QTIP) election to get the marital deduction. However, if the second annuitant is someone other than a spouse and survives the donor-annuitant, the value of the survivor's interest is included in the donor's taxable estate.

Gift tax implications. When a donor funds a two-life gift annuity with his or her own property, gift tax implications can be avoided by retaining the right to revoke the survivor's interest in the donor's will.

Reporting to donor. At the time of the gift, the charity will provide the donor a tax deduction receipt, a gift annuity agreement, federal income tax information, and supporting tax computations.

The charity will provide the annuitant Form W-2P each January. Form W2-P reports total income payments made in the taxable year just ended and the tax implications.

Recommended for. This plan is generally for persons age 60 or over. The annual tax-free portion of the annuity payment makes the effective return appealing. This rather high rate of return coupled with the tax deduction in the year of the gift makes the gift annuity an attractive plan.

Plan 9—Pooled Income Fund

Brief description. Cash or property is irrevocably transferred by the donor to the foundation's Pooled Income Fund (for the benefit of the donor's charity) where it is invested with similar gifts from others. Each beneficiary receives his or her share of the pooled income fund's distributable income each year. The fund functions like a traditional mutual fund.

Acceptable gifts. $1,000 or more.

Beneficiary provision. One or two lives.

Rate of income. The annual rate of return paid is

equal to his or her share of the amount of distributable income in the pooled income fund. The fund is invested in bonds, stocks, or other suitable investments.

Current tax benefits.

• The amount paid to each beneficiary is taxable as ordinary income.

• The gift transfer entitles the donor to a charitable deduction in the year of the gift. The size of the deduction is based on the age of the beneficiary(ies) at the time of the gift, the percent return paid to the donor, and the amount of money or fair market value of the property transferred to the pooled income fund.

• If the pooled income fund is funded with *cash*, the ceiling on the deduction is 50 percent of the donor's adjusted gross income with a five-year carryover for any excess.

• If the pooled income fund is funded with long-term *appreciated property*, the ceiling on the deduction is 30 percent of the donor's adjusted gross income with a five-year carryover for any excess.

Capital gains implications. No capital gain is generated on the gift transfer of long-term appreciated property to fund a pooled income fund. However, the alternative minimum tax may apply if the gift property is highly appreciated and the donor has a high income.

Estate tax implications. A one-life pooled income fund for the donor's life is completely excluded from his or her estate.

In a two-life pooled income fund, if the second income beneficiary is the spouse of the donor, the spouse's interest is not included in the donor's taxable estate if the executor makes a Qualified Terminable Interest Property (QTIP) election to get the marital deduction. If the second life income beneficiary is not a spouse, the value of the beneficiary's right to income is included in the donor's taxable estate.

Gift tax implications. When donors fund a two-life pooled income fund with their own separate property, they can avoid gift tax by retaining the right to revoke the survivor's interest in the donor's will.

Reporting to donor.

• At the time of the gift, the charity and the foundation provide the donor a tax-deductible receipt, a pooled income agreement, the plan, a disclosure statement, federal gift tax information and supporting tax computations.

• The foundation provides the income beneficiary Schedule K-1 (Form 1041) and the complete annual financial statement of the fund.

Recommended for. This plan is for donors who have less than $10,000 to invest and are interested in diversifying their investment risk for a relatively high yield.

Plan 10—Charitable Remainder Annuity Trust

Brief description. Cash or property is irrevocably transferred by the donor to the foundation of the donor's denomination or to the trustee of the donor's choice. These trustees invest and reinvest the assets in a separate fund for the benefit of the designated charity and the donor. The beneficiary receives a fixed dollar amount annually, which cannot be less than 5 percent of the initial fair market value of the transferred property.

Acceptable gifts. Cash or marketable securities.

Suggested amount. $10,000 or more.

Beneficiary provision. Usually it should not be for more than two lives unless the annuity trust is for a specific term of years instead of life.

Rate of income. The annual rate of return paid to the donor is negotiated at the time of the gift and remains constant for the life of the annuity trust.

Current tax benefits.

1. The income paid to the donor retains the character it had in the trust. Each income payment is treated:

• As *ordinary income* to the extent of the trust's ordinary income for the year (and any undistributed ordinary income from prior years);

• As *capital gain* to the extent of the trust's capital gain for the year (and any undistributed capital gains from prior years);

• As so-called *other income* (tax-exempt income) to the extent of the trust's exempt income for the year (and any undistributed exempt income from prior years); or

• As a *tax-free distribution of principal.*

2. The gift transfer entitles the donor to a charitable deduction in the year of the gift. The size of the deduction is based on the age of the income beneficiary(ies) at the time of the gift, the percent to be paid, and the amount of money or fair market value of the property transferred to the annuity trust.

• If the annuity trust is funded with *cash,* the ceiling on the deduction is 50 percent of the donor's adjusted gross income with a five-year carryover for any excess.

• If the annuity trust is funded with long-term *appreciated property,* the ceiling on the deduction is 30 percent of the donor's adjusted gross income with a five-year carryover for any excess.

Capital gain implication. No capital gain is incurred on the gift transfer of long-term appreciated property. However, the alternative minimum tax may apply if the gift property is highly appreciated and the donor has a high income.

Estate tax implications. A one-life annuity trust for the donor's life is completely excluded from his or her estate.

In a two-life annuity trust, if the second annuitant is the spouse of the donor, the spouse's interest is not included in the donor's taxable estate. However, if the second annuitant is someone other than a spouse and the donor survives the annuitant, the value of the survivor's interest is included in the donor's taxable estate.

Gift tax implications. When a donor funds a two-life annuity trust with his or her own separate property, gift tax implications can be avoided by retaining the right to revoke the survivor's interest by the donor's will.

Reporting to donor.

- At the time of the gift, the charity and the foundation provide the donor a tax deduction receipt, a charitable remainder annuity trust agreement, federal income tax information, federal gift tax information, and supporting tax computations.

- The foundation provides the income beneficiary Schedule K-1 (Form 1041) and a complete annual financial statement of the fund. Schedule K-1 (Form 1041) reports total income payments made in the taxable year just ended.

Recommended for. This plan is for donors with charitable interests who have highly appreciated low-yield assets and who wish to receive a quarterly fixed income for life.

Plan 11—Deferred Payment Gift Annuity

Brief description. Cash or property is irrevocably transferred to the donor's charity for the promise to pay a fixed amount annually to the donor for life, starting at a date more than one year from the gift transfer. For example:

Deferred Payment Gift Annuity

One-life, age 50

Lifetime payments begin at	65	70
Annual payment rate	13.30%	17.20%
Income tax-free (projected)	7.03%	4.20%
Immediate tax deduction	81.21%	88.37%
Effective yield 28% bracket	17.21%	22.86%

Two-life, age 50

Annual payment rate	12.40%	15.70%
Income tax-free (projected)	7.53%	4.75%
Immediate tax deduction	76.54%	84.58%
Effective yield 28% bracket	15.78%	20.57%

Acceptable gifts. Cash or marketable securities.

Suggested amount. The minimum gift is $2,000. The donor may repeat this gift on a yearly basis for several years as long as the donor wishes.

Beneficiary provision. The donor can name one or two beneficiaries. Usually they are the donor and his or her spouse, or the donor and some other person.

Rate of payments. The annual rate of return depends on the age of the income beneficiary(ies) at the time of the gift and on how long the donor defers the annuity payments. The annual rate of return then remains constant for life.

Current tax benefits.

• A portion of each annuity payment to the donor is tax free. This is similar to the gift annuity (Plan 8).

• The gift entitles the donor to a charitable tax deduction in the year of the gift. The size of the deduction is based on the age of the beneficiary(ies) at the time of the gift and on how long the donor defers income payments.

• If the deferred payment gift annuity is funded with *cash*, the ceiling on the deduction is 50 percent of the donor's adjusted gross income with a five-year carryover for any excess.

• If the deferred payment gift annuity is funded with long-term *appreciated property*, the ceiling on the deduction is 30 percent of the donor's adjusted gross income with a five-year carryover for any excess.

Capital gains implications. For a gift of appreciated property held long-term, the capital gain on only the investment portion of the deferred payment gift annuity is reported and spread over the donor annuitant's life expectancy, starting when the annuity payments begin. However, the alternative minimum tax may apply. This is similar to the gift annuity (Plan 8).

Estate tax implications.

• A one-life deferred payment gift annuity is excluded from the donor's estate, which may reduce federal estate taxes.

• In a two-life deferred payment gift annuity, if the second annuitant is the spouse of the donor, the spouse's interest is not included in the donor's taxable estate if the executor makes a Qualified Terminable Interest Property (QTIP) election to get the marital deduction. However, if the second annuitant is someone other than a spouse and survives the donor-annuitant, the value of the survivor's interest is included in the donor's taxable estate.

Gift tax implications. When a donor funds a two-life deferred payment gift annuity with his or her own property, gift tax implications can be avoided by retaining the right to revoke the survivor's interest in the donor's will.

Reporting to donor.

• At the time of the gift, the charity will provide the donor a tax deduction receipt, a deferred payment gift annuity agreement, federal income tax information, and supporting tax computations.

• Once income payments have begun, the charity provides the annuitant Form W-2P each January. Form W-2P reports total income payments made in the taxable year just ended and the tax implications.

Recommended for. This plan is for middle-aged persons with high incomes who want to shelter some current income until retirement. It also works well for younger persons who receive an inheritance and want to preserve the gift for a pensionlike income at age 65 or some future date.

The effective rate of return on this plan can be substantial. Check with your charity personnel for a workup based on your situation.

Plan 12—Charitable Remainder Unitrust

Brief description. A donor transfers money or property irrevocably to his or her denomination's foundation or to the trustee of the donor's choice. This person serves as a trustee for the benefit of the designated charity and the donor. The foundation invests and reinvests the assets in a separate fund. The beneficiary receives an income each year determined by multiplying a negotiated percent (which cannot be less than 5 percent) by the annual fair market value of the trust's assets.

A variation. The trust annually pays the beneficiary only the income that the trust generates up to the agreed-upon percent. Deficiencies created by income payments that are less than the percent in the unitrust agreement may be made up in later years. This variation allows for gifts of real estate that may not generate much income until the land is sold and the sale proceeds reinvested.

Because the income payments are based on an annual valuation of the trust assets, the income may increase or decrease over the years. If inflation and high interest rates continue, income will increase as the unitrust value increases.

Acceptable gifts. Cash, marketable securities, and real estate.

Suggested amount. $10,000 or more.

Beneficiary provision. It should not be for more than two lives unless the unitrust is for a fixed term of years. (This is in contrast to an agreement for life.)

Rate of income. The annual rate of return (5 percent or more) is negotiated at the time of the gift. The annual income is determined by the negotiated rate multiplied by the fair market value of the trust. The latter must be computed annually. If the trust agreement uses the variation type of "income only," then makeup payments will be made when there is enough income to make it possible.

Current tax benefits.

1. The amount paid to the income beneficiary retains the character it had in the trust. For example, each income payment is taxed:

• As *ordinary income* to the extent of the trust's ordinary income for the year (and any undistributed ordinary income from prior years);

• As *capital gain* to the extent of the trust's capital gain for the year (and any undistributed capital gains from prior years);

• As so-called *other income* (tax-exempt income) to the extent of the trust's exempt income for the year (and any undistributed exempt income from prior years);

• As a *tax-free distribution of principal.*

2. The gift transfer entitles the donor to a charitable deduction in the year of the gift. The size of the deduction is based on the age of the beneficiary(ies) at the time of the gift, the percent return to be paid to the donor, and the amount of money or fair market value of the property transferred to the unitrust.

• If the unitrust is funded with *cash*, the ceiling on the deduction is 50 percent of the donor's adjusted gross income with a five-year carryover from any excess.

• If the unitrust is funded with long-term *appreciated property*, the ceiling on the deduction is 30 percent of the donor's adjusted gross income with a five-year carryover for any excess.

Capital gain implications. No capital gain is generated on the gift transfer of long-term appreciated property to fund a unitrust. However, the alternative minimum tax may apply if the gift property is highly appreciated and the donor has a high income.

Estate tax implications.

• A one-life unitrust is excluded from the donor's estate.

• In a two-life unitrust, if the second life is the donor's spouse, the spouse's interest is not included in the donor's taxable estate. However, if the second beneficiary is someone other than a spouse and survives the donor-beneficiary, the value of the survivor's right to life-income payment is subject to tax in the donor's estate.

Gift tax implications. When a donor funds a two-life unitrust with his or her own separate property, gift tax can be avoided by retaining the right to revoke the survivor's interest by the donor's will.

Reporting to donor.

• At the time of the giving, the charity and the foundation provide the donor a tax-deductible receipt, a charitable remainder unitrust agreement, federal income tax information, federal gift tax information, and supporting tax computations.

• The foundation provides the income beneficiary Schedule K-1 (Form 1041) and a complete annual financial statement of the fund. Schedule K-1 (Form 1041) reports total income payments made in the taxable year just ended.

Recommended for. This plan is for donors who have highly appreciated assets, such as stock or real estate, with a low yield. It is also for donors whose assets will grow due to inflation. With this plan, the annual income will fluctuate, depending on growth of the trust assets.

Plan 13—Gifts Through a Will

Brief description. A will is simply a document you set up during your life to arrange for the disposition of the property you own at your death.

Your will can save your estate the cost of a court-appointed administrator. If you die intestate (i.e., without a will), your property is distributed according to the laws of the state in which you lived. Your plans or intentions are not considered. *Without a will none of your estate can be distributed to charity.*

Times to consider changing your will. There are a number of periods in life when you should review your will to be sure it meets your needs and expectations:

- A change in the makeup of the family;
- A material change in the nature or amount of the family's assets;
- A change in applicable state or federal law (which have been occurring every couple of years);
- A change in your priorities or interests. In a word, it's important to keep your will up to date.

Ways of naming your charity(ies). There are several ways to make a bequest to your charity(ies). You can leave a certain percentage of your estate or a specific amount of money. (A percentage figure is recommended.) You can also leave what remains of your estate after you have provided for those persons close to you. Or you can name your charity as the contingent beneficiary in your will. This means that your charity will receive money from your estate only if the other named beneficiaries in your will die before you. Finally, you may wish to designate your denomination's foundation as beneficiary of all your charitable bequests and then instruct the foundation how to disburse the funds.

Estate tax implication. By putting your charity in your will, you put your estate in a lower federal estate tax bracket. Thus you conserve your family's interest at the same time you help your charity.

Any size bequest appreciated. Some persons think that since they cannot make a large bequest, they need not include a charity in their will. Your charity appreciates a bequest of any size. A bequest to your charity symbolizes your desire to perpetuate your values and beliefs.

Suggested wording to make a bequest. A will is a legal document and should not be written without the aid of an attorney. When you meet with your attorney to write your will, be sure you have the correct legal names and addresses of the charities you want to name. If there are certain programs you want to name, it may be well to share this with the charity so your information is up to date when you meet with the attorney.

Recommended for. Everyone should have an up-to-date will at all times. While Plans 2 through 12 are applicable to selected persons, Plan 13 is a must for all. Furthermore, there is no way to practice Jubilee without a will. This is your last opportunity to make a statement about the values that have governed your life. Through your will you can advance the kingdom of God.

A Final Word

In all the descriptions above, most tax rates and tables have been omitted. Where numbers and percentage rates do appear, they are illustrations as of 1987, based on the 1986 tax law. If one of the thirteen plans seems useful to you, consult your financial counselor, your denominational foundation office, or the charity of your choice. They will help you with the current and up-to-date numbers based on the country in which you live, the most recent tax rates, your birth dates, and tax bracket.

Some of these procedures may seem complicated. However, by working through the processes, some of you will be able to increase your income while you are living, and at death transfer more to charity than you ever would have believed possible. It is worth going through the process to discover the possibilities.

The Scriptures encourage us to be faithful and obedient. If we are dilatory in our search for financial solutions, what kind of stewards of the gospel are we?

Pastors and other congregational leaders will want to be informed on the creative ways some of their members can be more involved in financing the church. Attendance at a denominational charitable foundation seminar on these deferred giving techniques will enable congregational leaders to be better counselors to their members. This is a positive way to teach the use of money for kingdom-building purposes. Church members joyfully respond to positive suggestions and teachings. These same members are pleased when they feel their congregational leadership is informed on these more sophisticated techniques.

8

Teaching Stewardship in the Congregation

T. A. KANTONEN, a Lutheran theologian, has long been a mentor to me through his writings. In his book, *A Theology for Christian Stewardship*, he writes:[1]

> If it [stewardship] represents only clever means which practical-minded Americans have devised for raising money, interest in it soon subsides. But if it can be shown to be vital Christian faith in action, revealing its power to transform all areas of life, then it raises the hope that here may be the beginning of a new awakening and renewal, a new coming of the Spirit.   (p. vii)

> The stewardship program of the church, if it is deeply rooted in living theology, may come to have the same significance for the twentieth century that the revival of world missions had for the nineteenth century. (p. 1)

> When the concept of stewardship is developed in its New Testament context it implies even more than trusteeship and responsibility. It contains the idea of partnership. The relation between master and servant

---

1. Fortress Press, Philadelphia, 1956.

gives way to the relation between friends working together for the realization of a common purpose. Thus in speaking to his disciples about their stewardship responsibility of fruitful service, our Lord says, "No longer do I call you servants, for the servant does not know what his master is doing; but I have called you friends, for all that I heard from my Father I have made known to you" (John 15:15, RSV).   (p. 4)

These three quotes establish a dream, a vision, and a reason for a strong and vibrant stewardship teaching program within the local congregation. Let us look more closely at Kantonen's key ideas.

- Stewardship is vital Christian faith in action, he says. It has power to transform all areas of life.
- It is the beginning of a new awakening and renewal, a new coming of the Spirit.
- If stewardship is deeply rooted in a living theology, it will have the same significance for the twentieth century as world missions had in the nineteenth century.
- Stewardship contains the idea of partnership, master and servant becoming friends, working together for the realization of a common purpose.

Not many persons see stewardship as an avenue for the awakening or the renewal of the church. Yet this renewal depends upon how the local congregation understands and teaches the idea. If we are stewards or managers of the gospel whose mission it is to continue the work Christ began . . . if Jesus has elected each of us to be his spokesperson . . . if he has given to each of us some working tools (time, abilities, money) to perform this task . . . if one day he will have a personal job performance review with each of us . . . then the local congregation holds a strategic teaching position. Isn't it true that most of us develop our vision and mission for the church from our congregational friends, teachers, role models, and mentors?

Although the church has been effective in the past, there is no doubt that a new and vibrant stewardship teaching plan can improve our obedience and our faithfulness. What does it take to improve teaching methods in our congregations? I am sure there is no *one* way. Certainly it will take the work of all faithful church members putting their efforts together into a workable plan for the congregation.

An Invitation to Adventure

The remainder of this chapter is to serve as an idea starter or a guide to this spiritual adventure. Perhaps your congregation can be a part of an exciting journey into a new realm. I hope your adventure leads you to the discovery of new opportunities for your congregation. There may be tests of faith. Certainly Christ's lordship and our own submissiveness will be examined. There will be self-examination, repentance, rededication, discipleship, and stewardship. This adventure can be, as Kantonen suggested, a deep, renewing experience.

The suggestions given here must be coordinated with procedures already in place in your congregation and with the counsel you receive from your district and national denominational offices. Congregational leadership must review the wide range of options and procedures, then design a strategic teaching plan appropriate for your church. No one knows the forces at work in your congregation better than your leadership team.

Above all, remember that teaching begins with *lead-*

ership and ends in a *total program performance review.* What follows are important steps in the realization of this renewal.

The Leadership Team

We normally think of the pastor as the congregational leader. But the pastor is not alone. A team of persons participates in the planning and execution of all programs. Team members frequently include the pastoral team, elders, Christian education leadership, the treasurer, and several strong leaders from the business and professional community. This team must come into agreement about style, approach, message, and goals. There are various approaches to designing a long-range plan, but listed here are several key steps that must be addressed by the leadership group.

The Importance of Goals

True stewardship insists on a visible evidence of faith. Stewardship is what one does after one says, "I believe." Spiritual values, such as the fruit of the Spirit (Gal. 5:22-23), operate only in specific actions in daily life.

The apostle John points out that we can measure our love for another person by the way we react to that person's need (1 John 3:17-18). In other words, stewardship is a measurement of our love for God. The New Testament emphasizes fruits, results, and actions as the test of faith. Jesus made this clear in the Sermon on the Mount. He said, "Not everyone who says to me, 'Lord, Lord,' will enter the kingdom of heaven, but only he who does the will of my Father who is in heaven" (Matt. 7:21).

The goal of stewardship teaching should be the winning of people to live a consecrated life, the beginning point of which is redemption through Christ. We are bought with a price. We, and all we have, are Christ's. As such, stewardship is not optional for a Christian. The only question is, Are we good or poor stewards?

Therefore, the goal of a congregational long-range stewardship program may be expressed like this.

> To confront the members of (name your congregation here) with God's call to responsibility for the gospel, to the end that persons may respond faithfully by (1) making available the resources divinely entrusted to them; and (2) by being personally involved in continuing the work Christ began in the world.

As you will observe, this goal is a summary of Chapters 2 through 6. If it's not applicable to your congregation, your leadership group can alter it. But the fact remains: The selection of a stewardship goal is the place to begin.

Mission Statement

Growing out of your stewardship teaching goal will be your long-term congregational mission statement. Again, you should look to your district and national church leadership for counsel on this matter. Your mission statement is the most important document the congregation will put together. Once accepted, it will influence each of the congregation's intermediate plans and the steps to put the plans into action.

With the congregation's stewardship goal and a mission statement in place, you are ready to look at how to establish a strategic plan to arrive at your mission, say ten years from now.

Strategic Planning[2]

For some members the terms *mission statement, strategic planning,* and *goal setting* may sound mechanical and manipulative—certainly not church-related. Terms such as *vision* and *dream* might be more palatable and say the same thing. Invite your members to help you grow into that dream and vision for the congregation. Everyone wants to help people grow and live into God's plan for their lives. Nothing just happens. An event results from a combination of forces. The schoolteacher makes a lesson plan for the next day, week, or month. The farmer plans crop rotation, soil improvements, and a livestock feeding program to reach his objectives. The church will fulfill its mission only when it plans a program which reflects the priority of living the gospel.

But how can the church fulfill its mission if each member proceeds with an individually oriented and independent approach to church work? Good planning contributes to satisfying results. Jesus gave many illustrations on the importance of planning, as in Luke 14:28-29: "Suppose one of you wants to build a tower. Will he not first sit down and estimate the cost to see if he has enough money to complete it? For if he lays the foundation and is not able to finish it, everyone who sees it will ridicule him."

Some people unashamedly say that the church is doing quite well when it has paid all its bills. But as long as persons are hungry, diseased, in prison, poorly

---

2. See the prototype sample in Appendix A.

clothed, and bound in sin, the church is always in debt. As long as there are people, the great commission will speak loudly to us: "Therefore go and make disciples of all nations, baptizing them in the name of the Father and of the Son and of the Holy Spirit, and teaching them to obey everything I have commanded you" (Matt. 28:19-20).

The Pastor's Role

Support from the pastor is essential. The effectiveness of the stewardship program will be in direct relation to the inspiration he or she imparts to lay leaders. In Romans, Paul specifically points out the importance of the preacher to the proclamation of the gospel.

> How, then, can they call on the one they have not believed in? And how can they believe in the one of whom they have not heard? And how can they hear without someone preaching to them? And how can they preach unless they are sent? As it is written, "How beautiful are the feet of those who bring good news!"

> But not all the Israelites accepted the good news. For Isaiah says, "Lord, who has believed our message?" Consequently, faith comes from hearing the message, and the message is heard through the word of Christ. (Rom. 10:14-17)

The minister must recognize that a congregation can understand and appreciate the principles of Christian stewardship only by catching a vision of God in action and by obeying that vision. This must constantly be kept before the congregation in a year-round plan. Waldo J. Werning, a stewardship teacher in the Lutheran tradition, believes a six- to nine-week series of sermons is essential to make a difference in peoples' lives. He says:

> Through sermons and field testing we have learned the importance of using a concentrated period of time to build understanding and interest. Six to nine Sundays are scheduled for this conditioning phase, at which time sermons, Bible studies, lay talks and children's object lessons are presented. . . . You may question such a comprehensive plan of education. Please keep in mind the biblical principle by the Holy Spirit, "Sow a little, reap a little; sow a lot, reap a lot." We have discovered that those who have faithfully sown the seeds of God's word in a six- to nine-week educational program have seen a drastic change of understanding, attitude and action on the part of Christian stewards.[3]

During the annual program-building and commitment period, the pastor should give added emphasis to the financial components of Christian stewardship. About one out of every six verses in the first three gospels concerns how we use material possessions. Nearly half of Jesus' parables deal with the responsibility of things that God has entrusted to us. The pastor must be well-versed on the *complete* subject of Christian stewardship, showing the relationship of material possessions to our stewardship of the gospel.

In addition to preaching, the pastor should see that the meaning of Christian stewardship is taught in Sunday school and other teaching media of the congregation.

Due to a rediscovery of the theological implications of stewardship, many fine books are available for the

---

3. Waldo J. Werning, *Supply-Side Stewardship* (Concordia Press, St. Louis. 1986), p. 98.

pastor's study. Your denominational stewardship office will bring the current and classical writings to the attention of the pastor each year. The pastor will find the following books helpful for depth studies in the field of Christian stewardship: Goldberg and Lewis's *Money Madness*; Kantonen's *A Theology for Christian Stewardship*; Kauffman's *Stewards of God*; Lederach's *A Third Way*; Piper's *The Christian Meaning of Money*; Powell's *Money and the Church*; Ralston's *Stewardship in the New Testament*; Stewart's *Thine Is the Kingdom*; Thompson's *Stewardship in Contemporary Theology*; Trueblood's *The Company of the Committed*; Werning's *Christian Stewards*; and Werning's *Supply-Side Stewardship*.

The pastor will have many opportunities to lead devotional studies using some of the following ideas:

Stewardship in the Lord's parables. The rich fool, the pounds, the talents, the good Samaritan, the wise and foolish virgins, the rich man and his steward, the creditor and the two debtors, the great supper, the unjust steward, and many more.

Basic stewardship teachings of our Lord. The importance of service (Matt. 25:32-46); the widow's mite (Luke 21:1-4); the Sermon on the Mount (particularly Matt. 6); commitment (John 21:1-20); confrontation (John 3:1-20); witness (Acts 1:8).

Stewardship studies in Paul's epistle. Many of Paul's letters deal with stewardship. Romans 12:1-11 treats the stewardship of ability and intellect. First Corinthians 12:1-12 is a similar passage on stewardship of time and talents. Romans 13:8-10 talks about the debt of love. First Corinthians 16:1-2 explains the basic pattern for New Testament proportionate giving. Second Corinthians 8 and 9 contain a whole section on the right motivation for Christian stewardship of self, service, and possessions. First Thessalonians 2:4; 2 Corinthians 5:19-20; 1 Corinthians 4:1; and Ephesians 3:10 talk about the stewardship of the gospel. Ephesians 2 and 4 deal with stewardship of occupation and vocation.

The list could go on and on! Stewardship committees have almost limitless resources at hand to develop a growing consciousness of stewardship in the congregation.

The Year-Round Task: It Takes More Than Preaching

We need to find many ways to connect our theology to the bread-and-butter issues our people face. If our theology doesn't intersect with life's problems, it is meaningless.

That is why there must be an increasing emphasis on stewardship education for all ages within the church. People must be helped to find answers to such questions as, Who am I? To whom am I responsible? Why should I give to the church? How much should I give? Do my time and abilities count? What is the relationship of my commitment to Christ and the church to my work, community membership, neighbors, and friends? Is the verbalization of my faith and experience a necessary part of being a steward? Does it matter how I spend the money I don't give to the church? Why should I make an annual commitment for a weekly gift to the church? What does it mean to be a steward of the gospel at home, at school, in the community, and in the church?

It is not the purpose of this chapter to answer these questions. What we are concerned with here is how one can introduce stewardship education into the life of the congregation.

Psychologists have told us for years that most learning takes place by observation. For that reason the learning environment for young people is crucial. The people who surround us determine who we are. They determine our values, our lifestyle, our priorities. It may well be profitable for young people to hear the life or faith stories of congregational members. Through these stories people learn how others have faced issues and why they made decisions as they did. Consider establishing fellowship groups if you don't have them now. These support groups are vital to congregational solidarity.

Our children, youth, and adults who use our denominational materials and church periodicals are exposed to much good stewardship education. In addition, there are other avenues which your leadership should use for stewardship education. Here are some supplemental ideas.

(1) Use the Sunday *church bulletin* and a church *newsletter* to report stewardship ideas, quotations from Scripture, and interpretative materials from our mission boards, conferences, colleges, seminaries, and other church organizations.

(2) Prepare *displays* on stewardship for the bulletin boards of the church.

(3) Secure *stewardship leaflets* for distribution to families a number of times each year. Integrate the distribution with stewardship sermons and other special emphases. The leaflets become "afterburners" for the sermon.

(4) Encourage the various organizations of the church to *build programs* around stewardship themes several times a year.

(5) Use *audiovisual aids, motion pictures,* and *film-strips.* They can be effective to open discussion on var-

ious phases of stewardship. An up-to-date listing is available from the denominational stewardship office.

(6) Encourage the library committee to place *good stewardship books* in the church library. Be sure to publicize the books from time to time. The denominational stewardship office can recommend good books.

(7) Make use of *study courses* suggested by the stewardship office for children's classes and youth and adult groups. Special study groups, midweek classes, Sunday evening study groups, or Sunday school classes will benefit by concentrating for a time in the area of stewardship.

(8) Suggest to planners the use of *stewardship skits* at appropriate times during the year. The stewardship office can make recommendations.

(9) Encourage your pastor to *emphasize stewardship* in *training* new church members, *preaching* stewardship sermons, *speaking* to children's stewardship issues, and *receiving the offering* on Sunday morning.

(10) Plan a *weekend stewardship conference* every three to five years to do special education in Christian stewardship.

(11) Use the *Christian Family and Money Management program,* which emphasizes responsibility for the total use of money and its priority in the stewardship of the gospel. Your denominational stewardship office will have its own suggestions, though you may consider the Roy and Lillian Bair materials. (See the bibliography.)

(12) Hold up *standards of giving* (including the tithe) before the congregation. There is no one standard of giving appropriate to all persons in all circumstances and at all times. Persons must develop a standard for themselves which they can test with their trusted peers and reconcile with their consciences before God.

The consumer drive in each of us makes us want to respond to secular consumer practices. That is why each of us needs the support of our community of faith to help us see ourselves in our temptations and resulting decisions.

To be able to share our income and giving plans with trusted friends makes us vulnerable. But this experience has proven helpful again and again. If your members are not ready for this step, a few could try it and share their experiences and feelings with the rest. Later, others can try the sharing when they are ready to allow the community of faith to speak to them about this personal response.

The first step in developing such a standard is to realize we are responsible to God for the proper use of our total income.

The second step is to consider what is a worthy proportion of our total income to allocate to the maintenance and extension of Christ's church on earth, to the relief of poverty and suffering, and to the assistance of others.

Most people like to decide on a percentage of their income to commit to charitable causes. This then becomes the firstfruits portion of their income set aside for God's work.

Having decided upon the total amount they wish to give, persons must next decide for themselves how much they will give through the church and how much to other causes. In normal circumstances, the amount given to all church purposes should be the substantial portion of the total.

The committed amount should be a first priority for distribution from income. That is why we call it firstfruits.

These decisions should be made annually. In making

these firstfruit decisions we should remember that we are members within a congregation—each member assuming some responsibility for the others' growth and development. As suggested above, many have found it helpful to share their giving plans with trusted friends within their fellowship of believers.

Note also, the principles of stewardship apply to accumulations of capital as they do to current income. One should not overlook the importance of giving out of capital, whether during life or by bequest.

(13) Select *mentors* for youth. Role models and heroes have a profound influence on all of us. Too often youth's mentors are self-selected from the secular world. Consider having your 10- to 17-year-olds select mentors from within the congregation who can spend time with them. A young person wanting to be an entrepreneur can spend time with a businessperson. The one dreaming to be a nurse can be assigned to a nurse. The same with would-be teachers, doctors, lawyers, farmers, truckers, and builders. Naturally, the mentors selected should be stewardship models also. This selection can have a profound influence on a young life.

(14) Attend *training seminars.* From time to time your denomination will plan motivational and teaching seminars. These meetings are always "sight raisers." Arranging to have a number of your leadership team present for these seminars is another way to work at in-service training. Also, there are periodic interdenominational stewardship seminars planned by the Department of Stewardship of the National Council of Churches. These National Council seminars are planned for denomination leaders. However, if you have potential district or national leaders within your congregation, attendance at these seminars is a good

way to enlarge their horizons and to prepare them to become congregational leaders in future years.

(15) Work at *church mission interpretation.* The purpose of interpreting the church's mission is to help members develop a sense of involvement and to accept personal responsibility for the congregation's local and worldwide mission. Some how-to suggestions follow.

Use leaflets and brochures describing the various aspects of the general mission of the church by mailing them to the congregation, by placing them in the families' literature boxes, or by supplying the literature racks.

Show films, videos, and filmstrips describing and interpreting the work the church is doing to express her mission.

Plan Sunday evening programs to interpret the work of the district and national programs of your denomination, including the work of publishing, mutual aid, colleges, missions, congregational ministries, relief and service, and camping.

Invite missionaries, fraternal delegates, relief and service personnel, and overseas nationals to speak in church services or to organizations. For suggestions on who is available, write to the district and national boards of your denomination.

Invite students and faculty members from your church colleges and seminaries to visit your congregation to share their experiences and to interpret the work of these important church institutions.

Plan for tour groups from your congregation to visit social service centers, church planting and development projects, inner-city churches, hospitals, schools, mission boards, publishing centers, mutual aid centers, and other places where your church has work.

Ask the congregation to use the denomination's

annual mission education materials.

Ask the pastor to emphasize and interpret the total program of the church in *sermons* (including children's sermons), *prayers* at the time of receiving the offering, *talks* to organizations within the church, and in the use of *minute* people. Minute people are members who are asked to study recent happenings at a specific mission point and then give a one-minute report to the congregation. This is effectively done just before the offering. The pastor can then add: Our offering this morning will strengthen this and many other causes in the church.

Use the Sunday bulletin and congregational newsletter to inform members of the church's program. In this reporting and in the use of minute people, remember that our colleges, other church institutions, and district conference are also our mission.

Set aside one area of the church for the interpretation of the church's program. Display large maps of the world and nations showing where missionaries and fraternal workers are located. Show pictures of mission personnel and provide cultural displays which will help the members understand overseas churches and peoples. As a variation, you could also have a special education month, showing on the map where your college alumni are in service. Your colleges will be glad to cooperate with you. Use tables and other means for displaying books, studies, models, reports, and other interesting items.

Plan an effective missions week each fall when missionary interpretation will reach all organizations. Use films, videos, leaflets, and speakers.

Be sure to teach new members the importance of the church's mission and give them an understanding of the scope of the denomination's program.

Suggest that your ministers pick out key items in the budgets of our various church organizations and report them in the church bulletin. This helps to relate the mission work and the cost to put that program into action.

Report weekly the gifts of money received. Do this through the church bulletin. The following form is a suggestion for you:

Offering last Sunday	$_____
Weekly amount needed for our approved program	$_____
Total received this year to date	$_____
Total amount needed this year to date	$_____

This weekly report keeps before the members the current financial situation of the congregation. They know whether they are behind or ahead of the plan as of any specific date.

Local Mission Opportunities

Churches often do not realize that missionary activities and opportunities are within easy reach of every congregation. These "local missions," such as a new church development or an inner-city church, may already be in operation. Your congregation can study and help these efforts.

Remember to provide hospitality to foreign students. There are over 100,000 foreign students in the United States at any given time. Since these foreign students will likely be leaders in their countries when they return home, relating to them can be some of the most effective mission work of the church.

Many local mission opportunities exist. One is providing hospitality to foreign students from our nearby colleges and universities. Another is assisting in the resettlement of refugees. One could care for seasonal migrants or reach out to minority groups. Think about assisting nearby church developments or inner-city churches. Assist at rescue missions or provide aid to social service projects.

Design a witness and visitation program sponsored by the congregation. It could be directed to neighbors and unchurched friends or to men and women with whom the local members work. Or one could begin Bible study groups at the YMCA (or other suitable place) for civic and industrial leaders of the community.

Some of these types of outreach do not have a cost to them, but if your local congregation is to fulfill its mission, they are important. The plans for following through should be a part of the congregation's program. These opportunities are not necessarily the responsibility of the stewardship committee unless assigned by the congregation.

The time and efforts members give to such projects are a part of their personal stewardship. Encourage the congregation to include some of the above or similar activities in the total program of the church. Part of the mission is also to recruit candidates and train them to become ministers, missionaries, fraternal workers, and faculty members within our school system.

Other Considerations

Program building. Planning the local program and developing a budget which contributes to the realization of that program involves stewardship principles.

When one spends funds on one project, one cannot use the same money for something else. Including nonessentials in a program, may mean leaving out something vital. Congregations which understand that program building demands good stewardship do better planning. This involves all organizations and groups within the congregation and is a process that takes place over a number of months.

Proper division of funds between local and general mission. Many congregations as well as individuals give only out of their surplus. They see first what is needed to carry out the local mission and make plans to meet this local need. After that, they may consider the general mission. In other words, if there is anything left over, the congregation then considers giving to causes beyond itself.

This plan, or lack of it, assumes that the local mission is more important than the general mission—that what we spend on our own congregation is our primary responsibility. The general board of your denomination likely has affirmed that both are equally important and has encouraged congregations to seek the highest possible level of giving. It has urged that congregations apply the idea of proportionate division of funds between the local and general mission. There are suggestions to guide a congregation in this distribution, but the final decision is up to the local congregation. This is called self-allocation. The congregation is a "self." The membership as a group makes the decision.

The local congregation might consider a four-point standard for the division of funds as follows:

• Each congregation should seek to reach the highest potential of giving for the general mission.

• On the way to achieving its highest potential, each congregation should first establish a ratio of one dollar for general mission to each two dollars spent for the local mission. This should be the goal of small congregations.

- It should then pass on to a dollar-for-dollar distribution. That is, for every dollar spent locally, a church should give a dollar to the church's general mission. This should be the goal for medium-sized congregations.

- After a congregation has reached its one-for-one ratio, it should press on toward the mark of a sixty-forty ratio: 60 percent for the church's general mission and 40 percent for local mission. This goal, or a higher one, should be for the larger congregations.

Bequests and special gifts. In each congregation there are persons of means who are able to give more than others. Often they may participate generously in support of specific projects in the local or global mission. Each church should have a strategy for approaching these individuals to challenge them to higher levels of giving.

Also, all members should be encouraged to remember the church in their wills and estate planning. Such a bequest program is a continuing witness to the faith of a member long after he or she is unable to express that faith personally. The stewardship committee should consider an estate-planning conference at least once each five years. The general board of your denomination, through its foundation or stewardship committees, is able to assist the local congregation in planning such a conference.

Use of questionable methods to raise money. The seeking of monetary commitments from congregational members must flow from the fundamental beliefs of our Christian faith as they relate to stewardship. We have briefly outlined these in the earlier chapters of this book. *Congregations must avoid less worthy motives at all cost!* Some of these are: (1) Everyone should do their fair share.[4] (2) A strong church is good for the town or community. (3) We receive back more than we give. (4) You will be respected (achieve status). (5) It is the thing to do. Everybody else is doing it (social pressure). (6) Your gift fights communism.

A word is also in order about money-making schemes and gimmicks in some congregations. These plans are evasions of the basic responsibility of Christians to give freely and generously out of a heart of love for what God has done for them. Congregations should be cautious about sales, bazaars, fairs, suppers, and other money-raising events. They may do permanent harm to congregations by replacing true biblical stewardship with commercial venture.

An adequate accounting system. An adequate system of accounting is most important for every church. Such a system should include the accounting of receipts and expenditures. The accounting system should include the recording of church members' giving to provide receipts for tax purposes.

The stewardship councils of most denominations have prepared a manual for church treasurers, giving specific steps for a treasurer to follow in keeping records.

Church offering envelopes. There probably is no item more effective in educating people to give regularly than the offering envelope. Here is a weekly reminder that the church comes first in one's planning. Every congregation should make offering envelopes available

---

4. While the concept of a fair share is noble, it is usually determined by the cost of the total project divided by the potential participants. This is not right. The fair share becomes too big for the poor and too mediocre for the wealthy. As a result it's not a fair share for anybody!

and encourage their use.

The weekly predated envelopes remind the church member of a missed Sunday and makes it possible for the church treasurer to issue a receipt at the close of the year. This receipt can be used for income tax deductions. A pack of fifty-two envelopes can be purchased from your church supply office at a reasonable price.

Nonresident members. Nearly every congregation has a number of its members living in other cities and countries. Given the opportunity, they probably still want to participate in the benevolence program of their home congregation. The pastor or the commitment chairman should prepare a special letter encouraging these members to send their tithes and offerings back to the home congregation. These persons should also be receiving other regular mailings to strengthen home ties.

Teach stewardship in reverse. Mary Cosby from the Church of the Savior in Washington, D.C., described one of the ministries in her congregation where the wealthy are invited to meet, listen to, and learn from the poor. The Bible is full of this kind of reverse missioning.

> God chose the foolish things of the world . . . the weak things . . . the lowly things . . . the despised things . . . the things that are not—to nullify the things that are, so that no one may boast before him. (1 Cor. 1:27-29)

Poor people do have something to give to rich people (that's me). When have you heard a stewardship sermon that did not assume the haves giving to the have-nots? What might happen if this were reversed and poor people would be empowered through patient love to share how subsisting on little affects their experience of life, faith, God, and relationships? It may not always be nice to hear. It could be profound and challenging. It might result in becoming rich—in spirit, in humility, in new perspective. (See Matt. 5:3 and 2 Cor. 8:9.)

> True Christian stewardship will not come as long as the flow of resources and learning is one way. It includes the awareness that my most essential stewardship is not of money, but of faith, hope, and love. It could involve dying and rising again. Know any examples?[5]

The Offering as the Climax of the Worship Service

In 1964 during one of the Stewardship Institutes referred to in Chapter 1, Paul M. Miller told us the churches in Africa frequently schedule the offering near the end of the worship service. He shared the rationale for this change. Later *Stewardship Facts* reprinted a portion of this message. I quote it here.

> Worship is a meeting of a person with the Almighty in which God comes in his holiness and grace, and in which a person responds with confession, trust, praise, giving and reconsecration. A person cannot fully present his or her body as a reasonable act of worship until the mercies of God have first been presented in all of their overwhelming power.
>
> For this reason the presenting of tithes and offerings as an act of worship to God should come late in the worship service. Certainly something so rich in sacred meaning should not be lost amidst opening announce-

---

5. James Lapp in *Gospel Herald*, March 24, 1987, p. 201.

ments. The offering should not be lifted apologetically as if it were a regrettable gimmick which the church invented as a way to get needed money.

Apparently the epistles in the New Testament gained their place in the canon of Holy Scripture partly because they were read so often as the central message of early Christian services of worship. Evidently the early Christians were called to consider the offering near the climax of the worship service because it is at this point that giving is mentioned in almost every epistle. (See Romans 15:14-28; 1 Corinthians 16:1; Galatians 6:7-10; Philippians 4:14-20; 1 Thessalonians 5:12-25; 1 Timothy 6:17-19.)

The call for any unredeemed person to come to Christ in surrender and faith should be given after the gospel of God's grace has been presented during the worship. The call for believers to present their bodies and their offerings anew to God is just as real a call, demanding just as real and definite a response, and should likewise be presented near the climax of the service.[6]

Performance Review

Certainly we don't need complex forms to evaluate at year's end how we have done. But people like to be affirmed and to discover their successful ventures along with their failures. The leadership team should spend one meeting reviewing successes and evaluating weaknesses. They should evaluate the steps one by one. The following Sunday, the pastor or a dedicated lay leader can report the findings to the congregation.

---

6. Paul M. Miller, *Stewardship Facts*, (Dept. of Stewardship and Benevolence, National Council of Churches, New York City, 1965-66), p. 54.

The steward's rewards come in many shapes and sizes. Each member will know how he or she has done personally. But having the pastor comment on a few specifics, including the naming of selected persons as an encouragement for others for next year, will be helpful.

9

Money and Economic Issues in the Congregation

1 Timothy 6:3-20; James 2:14-22; James 4:1-12

IN THE LAST chapter I shared suggestions on how to teach stewardship on a year-round basis. The suggested procedures involve all members of the congregation. For some the vision of this responsibility for the gospel will break through in a new way. Lights will go on. Possibilities will become real. Strategies will become active. Some will have an "aha" experience. That is, they will say, "Aha! Why haven't I thought of this before?" It will be as Kantonen said—a renewal experience.

We continue in this chapter with our "how-to" suggestions on teaching stewardship. But now we focus on a single, sensitive, and seldom-discussed component of stewardship in the congregation: economic issues in family and individual life. Most people do not bring their money problems to church with them. Yet, our total life is to be integrated into our mission to continue Christ's work. If we are to use our tools of time, abilities, and wealth in this task, how can we leave family economics out of our congregational teaching plan? We *must* find ways to include biblical values toward money and our uses of money in our congregational teaching and members' support networks. If we don't, we force our members to select their economic role models and lifestyle standards from the secular world.

An Experiment in 1980–81

In November 1979 John Rudy (a friend and fellow believer in the importance of stewardship) and I were discussing the alienation some Christians feel because of conflicts involving money. We both believed there ought to be more positive ways to speak about money, more ways to see it as an enabler of the gospel rather than a deterrent to one's faith and growth. We wanted to find ways to introduce the "Zacchaeus factor" spoken of in Chapter 3 of this book.

At that moment an idea was born! I had a sabbatical, beginning in September 1980, and John was making shifts in his managerial responsibilities at the Mennonite Foundation. During the next six months, we developed a plan for a year of experimental work among our congregations. We wanted to discover creative processes and models for serious congregational dialogue about money matters that would lead members to greater Christian obedience and faithfulness.

Our proposed experiment received the endorsement of the General Board of the Mennonite Church. Their blessing to us included the following statement:

> Renewal in the area of economic issues will need demonstration. We must proceed from the rhetoric of

criticism to the practical implementation of reform.

> We need an effective process which will lead our people to carefully examine economic issues, to make some decisions together, to take at least some mini-steps, to move toward personal and corporate commitment. The process, rather than leading to rules and regulations, should be designed to facilitate helpful confrontation among brothers and sisters at local congregational levels. The process should get people talking with each other about these matters of importance.[1]

The Mennonite Mutual Aid board became our sponsoring group, along with a special advisory subgroup of persons. These two groups worked with John and me in developing three objectives and three goals for the project.

The Objectives

(1) To provide helpful guidance and prophetic leadership in identifying and addressing the bewildering economic issues which confront Christians in their everyday lives.

(2) To solicit the help of persons throughout the church in developing a biblical understanding of money and to apply these biblical principles to the effective use of money in their family and church responsibilities.

(3) To design and encourage effective models and processes, together with whatever tools and materials may be needed, which help local congregations to enter into serious dialogue about money matters and to

---

1. *Money and Ecomomic Issues,* John Rudy and Daniel Kauffman (Mennonite Mutual Aid Association, Goshen, Ind., 1981), p. 3.

challenge each other to greater Christian obedience and faithfulness.

The Goals

(1) To identify the primary money and economic issues facing Mennonites during the 1980s.

(2) To compile a bibliography, selected study papers, and other resource materials for pastors, professors, church high school teachers, and other kinds of church teachers and lay persons interested in the subject.

(3) To design and test a variety of effective aids and processes which will help our people to examine carefully the economic issues, to make some decisions together, to take some ministers toward personal and corporate commitment. The aids are to be practical and useful in assisting church members to be faithful and obedient Christians in money matters.

Every project should have measurable outcomes. The desired *outcome* for this project was stated as follows:

> By the end of this special Task Force on Money and Economic Concerns, a process model will have developed to facilitate helpful confrontation and constructive dialogue among brothers and sisters at local congregational levels on sensitive issues of getting, keeping, using, and giving money. This outcome will be supported by the development of tools and materials which may be used in the church to continue to process in the immediate years ahead. The project should be seen *not* on the basis of what we *do to* the congregation or what we *do for* them. It is important that the project be centered on what we *do with* them.[2]

---

2. *Ibid.*, p. 3.

The Strategies

To achieve the objectives and goals listed above, we needed a work plan and an orderly approach that was congregationally oriented and tested. In September 1980 the work plan was stated as follows:

(1) About a dozen congregations will be selected from both the Mennonite and General Conference Mennonite Church. Intensive listening, teaching, experimenting, processing, "yes butting," and testing will be done. Congregations selected will covenant to work at the task over a series of months in a variety of settings.

(2) Existing congregational settings will be used. These will include Sunday and midweek meeting periods, Sunday school classes, boards of elders and/or church councils, K-groups, families, individuals, retreats, etc.

(3) The Kauffman-Rudy agenda will work at trying to help congregations find some answers to questions such as:

• In what ways can Christians motivate and affirm each other to greater Christian obedience and faithfulness in money matters?

• How can brothers and sisters help remove the blocks and obstacles for each other that keep them from expressing their Christian obedience and faithfulness in money matters (in the accumulation, use, and disposition of money)?

• What are the opportunities and dangers in our economic system?

• In what ways should a Christian's money behavior be influenced by biblical principles?

• How can brothers and sisters reduce their hesitance and fears of experiencing mutually helpful, non-legalistic dialogue on money matters?

• What are the obstacles to giving money a more conspicuous place on congregational agendas?

• What is the real significance of money? Is money you (your mind, skill, and brawn) in portable form? Can we see it as a value for self-expression? Can it be used as a self-reward to celebrate success, hard work, a period of testing, etc.? A way to share in an act of service and love? Any or all of the above?

• Should a congregation identify and commission "financial" ministers? Perhaps a new kind of deacon?

• How can we make it easier and less threatening to give and receive counsel so that individuals are better equipped to make good money decisions?

• What makes a good annual teaching program on money in the congregation?

• Are there "peer support groups" (within or outside the congregation) that business persons need to work at their common problems?

With these General Board blessings and the objectives, goals, and strategies, we began the project in September 1980. Eleven congregations were selected from Virginia, Pennsylvania, Ohio, Indiana, Illinois, Kansas, and Manitoba. These congregations identified seventeen money and economic issues. The twelve most frequently identified issues appear below in summary fashion and in the order of the frequency identified. Congregations asked for:

(1) Assistance with the basic biblical teaching and meaning of Christian stewardship.

(2) Help with personal and family money management.

(3) Establishment of some basic principles for estate planning.

(4) Assistance in resolving hindered fellowship and negative feeling in the congregation about money.

(5) Guidelines on establishing a responsible Christian lifestyle.

(6) Assistance in establishing "financial ministers" or deacons and deaconesses who can assist in resolving issues members feel deeply about. For instance, some widows feel overwhelmed by economic demands and decisions. Other persons feel alienation and guilt because of money. Some have an inadequate income to support their desired standard of living. Some fear losing their jobs. Others fear the impending bankruptcy of the Social Security system. Some are unable to buy a house. Yet others worry that their small business will not survive. Some are unable to make debt payments or have inadequate funds for their children's education. Some worry about potential high taxes related to transferring their farm or business upon their death. Some of those with money feel they are kept "on the fringes" of congregational life. Some worry about declining real estate values or the erosion of their savings due to inflation. Some wonder whether they will have an adequate retirement income. Some are amazed at the stupid things others say about business and finances. Sometimes members will balk at what they consider too much talk about living the simple life. Some do not appreciate church leaders who make people feel guilty about money. Others just want help to know how much is enough. Others believe the young people want too much too soon. Others see too many family arguments about money. Some persons would like counsel on how big a business or farm should become. Some would welcome lifetime career planning or counsel. Some would like help in knowing how to pass on a family business.

(7) Help in evaluating worthy and unworthy causes to which to give money.

(8) Guidelines for children on money values.

(9) Help in developing convictions to increase personal and family giving according to New Testament standards and firstfruits in the Old Testament.

(10) Help in understanding the entrepreneurial personality which is by nature self-confident, assertive, and risk-taking.

(11) Help in developing a prophetic dialogue with our church leaders, writers, and speakers so counsel can flow two ways.

(12) Help in developing more personal ownership in the unified program budget of the congregation.

All of the above represent opportunities for ministry in the local congregation—opportunities often missed.

No one congregation selected more than five issues to work through. Some had only four. But there were clearly live and vibrant interests involving this third tool God gave to use for kingdom-building purposes.

John Rudy and I had an interesting year. We were convinced that the time had come for our congregations to be more assertive in addressing money issues. We tried to work with each congregation in finding biblical and nonthreatening processes to resolve each of the twelve issues.

After the project was over (July 1981) Rudy and I edited a *Congregational Guidebook in Money and Economic Issues*. The book outlines the steps each congregation used in working through its identified issues. Later (1984) Rudy edited another helpful kit of 184 typewritten pages giving suggestions on ways congregations can respond to a wide area of stewardship and money issues. The Rudy kit of ideas is called "Christian Stewardship: Faith in Action," and contains two congregational case stories (First Mennonite, Richmond; and Bethel Mennonite, Winnipeg, Canada) on how each congregation worked at identifying their issues and what came of it.

Another resource to consider is the book entitled *Full Value*, also listed in the bibliography. I recommend it for discussion groups of interested businesspersons in the congregation, as well as for pastors who want to understand something of the economic and management issues their businesspersons face. The biblical values and stories in the first seventy-five pages will be invaluable for pastors as they prepare sermons on the complex business and economic issues faced by many persons in each congregation. The case stories in the last half of the book, taken from the *Wall Street Journal*, become the grist for the value applications in the book's first seventy-five pages.

A Final Word on Stewardship Education

The rewards of a forthright stewardship teaching-counseling program can be fulfilling. But remember, changes take place slowly. The first small step may seem only a change in externals. But later steps can create a whole new course for one's life. It was Peter who first left his nets—an external step. Later he experienced growth and maturity (Matt. 4:18-22). Sometimes we *act* our way into a new way of thinking rather than *think* our way into a new way of acting.

There are two simple educational learning principles that apply to this whole stewardship project: (1) Do what you can with what you have. (2) What you don't use, you will lose.

Both principles are obvious, but congregations have often passed over the second one. We talk about gift discernment but rarely identify skills in the area of money matters. As a result, we lose those skills in the church. With the suggestions in Chapters 8 and 9 you will identify many skills you didn't know were resident among your members.

In our stewardship teaching we need to translate our supreme value (Christ) into goals and actions. This deepens our hold on Christian values. Truth and belief must be lived into meaning. As John said in John 1:14: "The Word became flesh and made his dwelling among us." As each of us becomes obedient and faithful to Christ's teachings, we too will grow and mature as Peter did. Shouldn't this be our goal?

10

The Denomination's National and District Boards

Jude 1-25

WE NOW SHIFT our focus from the individual and the congregation to the denominational district and national boards. Our theology of stewardship remains the same, however. The individual and the congregation are still central. As said so often in this book, the gospel has been entrusted to believing individuals and the communities of Christian faith to continue Christ's work until he returns.

As these same individuals and communities of faith consider their national and global responsibilities, they begin to think organizationally. That is, they begin to search for ways to release some persons from the congregation for special tasks of ministry beyond the home areas. This requires a support system and a supervisory role. One must establish accountability to the congregation. With the beginning of district, national, and international offices, we meet that inevitable by-product of growth: bureaucracy.

It's easy for this bureaucracy to make people in the local pew feel that they exist for the support of the denominational boards, especially when boards and agencies get too free with crisis financial appeals. "Dig deeper!" they say, "or we'll have to bring missionaries home or close certain divisions!"

These kinds of crisis appeals are not effective in the long run. People respond to appeals from strength more than appeals from weakness. They prefer to support a movement, a cause, or an organization that gives hope and promise rather than failure. They want to believe your organization is helping persons become what God wants them to become. They don't want to be used, but rather to be helpers and facilitators of a mission that is administered well. If your people are caught up with the vision, they will volunteer to be a part of that mission through generous financial support!

Remember that local individuals brought the district and national boards into existence in the first place. Therefore, each national and district board has a responsibility to listen closely to the home folks. They should search out their individual convictions and dreams for the extended ministry of the church and plan a program that achieves these dreams. They should report to the supporting congregations the results of the boards' administration.

As soon as we develop bureaucracies, terms such as *public relations, marketing, fund-raising,* and *promotion* begin to appear. These are good and necessary procedures to keep local church members informed, yet sometimes the procedures appear more important than people and misunderstandings may develop on either side.

In theory, church relations for a church board

should grow out of the agency's reason for being. That is, to find ways and means to pool the efforts of many congregations for the larger ministry of the church. Good church relations develop through an exchange of the expectations, wants, and needs between the members of local congregations and the larger church agency. For example, a church agency needs advocates, prayers, and support. On the other hand, the local church members who respond also have wants and needs. They need to see evidence of productive and effective work from the agency. They want to be taken seriously as they make suggestions. They want to be recognized as important links to district, national, and world outreach.

One way for the church agency to recognize the individual donor's or congregation's needs is to personalize thank you letters for monetary contributions. Cite recent events of human interest in your ministry, illustrating how people have changed because of your efforts. Then you say, "Your contribution helped to make this possible." Personalize your acknowledgment further, so it wouldn't fit any person or congregation except the one to whom you are writing. People want to know they are important to your kingdom outreach. They want assurance that their gift is helping to continue your great cause. *Never* write a form letter that could apply to hundreds of people. Remember the Fosdick quote in Chapter 5. Money "is your personal energy reduced to portable form." That is why it is important to show that your agency is working as the "folks at home" would have you work.

One can diagram this notion that church relations is an exchange of needs as follows.

Good Church Relations

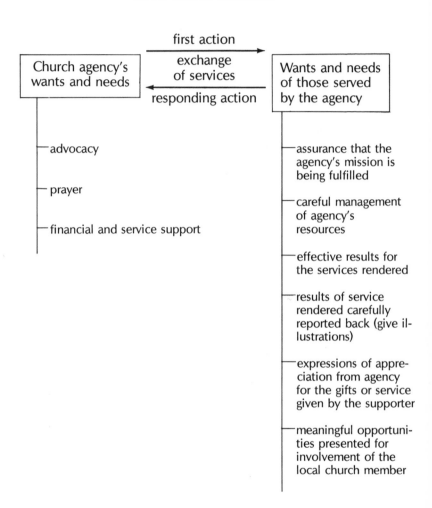

Diagram 7

In planning a church relations program, it is important that the district and national church board or agency take the first move. Otherwise the local church members will not respond by meeting the needs of the agency. Responding to each other's needs is certainly within the church's concern for brotherhood and mutual support.

The district and national boards need to identify the expectations of their supporting constituencies, recognizing that the needs of all local church members are not the same. The boards and agencies that serve well usually segment their various publics into natural groupings.

Most boards and agencies have the following natural groupings which we define as publics: children, youth, young single adults, young marrieds, singles, middle-age persons, persons fifty-five years and older, and pastors. Each agency must fine-tune the identified publics within the major groupings. For instance, a college board may segment the youth group into junior high, senior high, public and private high schools, and perhaps rural and metropolitan. A college services many community groups—business and industry, foundations, alumni, and a host of other friends. These are merely refinements of the grouping process so reporting can be directed to each group.

In determining your agency's various publics, remember the internal groups such as employees, families of employees, boards of directors, current students, and the other denominational board and agency networks of the church. These internal persons can become strong advocates for effectively communicating the mission of your agency to new areas.

The following page is a worksheet that may be helpful for an administrator of a board or an agency. The top half is self-explanatory. The bottom half is an expansion of the top half. Each public named should have the lower half filled out in its behalf. If you are an administrator, don't hesitate to dream a bit at this point. The ideas you list in the lower half of the sheet may be the difference between good or poor church relations for your agency.

Church relations done well will be unnoticed. But if an agency is crude and manipulative, its efforts can border on repulsive. The apostle Paul is a good model to follow. Each epistle has excellent examples of good church relations. Paul reports on the current work being done. He thanks people for their gifts. He shares opportunities for new avenues of service. He asks for continued support to manage his mission board. He compares one congregation's responses to another congregation's—Philippi with Corinth. And he holds forth a model for Christian living and expressions of the faith. These are examples of church relationships at their best.

I have spent most of my life on the side of the church board and agency—specifically in church colleges. At times I have observed some very irritated church members at the local level. They had a right to be irritated because we (the college) made mistakes. But I have had many more experiences where the congregations and the people were pleased with our reporting. When church relationships are going well, members of the local congregation want to help the district and denominational agencies achieve their mission. They become enthusiastic advocates with supporting words and finances. And at the end of their lives they want to leave a bequest for the mission or cause in which they had shown interest. But the last

Your Agency's Publics
(A Worksheet)

_____

Agency name

Internal publics   *External publics*

_____   _____
_____   _____
_____   _____
_____   _____
_____   _____
_____   _____
_____   _____
_____   _____
_____   _____
_____   _____

•   •   •

What does your agency offer to satisfy these needs?

Public: _____

Donor needs   *Services offered*

_____   _____
_____   _____
_____   _____
_____   _____
_____   _____
_____   _____
_____   _____
_____   _____

will and testament is left to your ministry only if the individual member feels good about your agency.

Finally, the work of the church must be a worldwide mission. A congregation in Indiana can serve in Africa, Asia, or Latin America only by making it possible for some members to go and serve. This requires supervision, boards, advocacy, and financial support. For all this to happen, good church relations on the part of the district and national boards are a must.

Note the book of Jude. The writer makes me want to be a part of his vision and ministry. At the same time Jude extends a hope and blessing to me. These are church relationships at their best. I urge you to read the entire chapter, but note especially the personal blessing in the final verses.

> To him who is able to keep you from falling and to present you before his glorious presence without fault and with great joy—to the only God our Savior be glory, majesty, power and authority, through Jesus Christ our Lord, before all ages, now and forevermore! Amen.
>
> (Jude 24-25)

Certainly those of us working for denominational boards and agencies can find ways to make our message contemporary so it has the same effect on our people as did the writings of the New Testament in the first century!

11

The Steward's Reward

Matthew 19:27-30
Matthew 25:21
Hebrews 11 (esp. 11:4, 13)

EACH OF US has been conditioned by our parents, our society, and our culture to look for certain rewards when we do a job well. As parents and grandparents, we enjoy doing things for our children and grandchildren. When they look up into our faces and give us that smile of appreciation, we love it. These are our rewards.

What are the rewards for our being faithful and obedient stewards of the gospel? This is a question much like Peter asked. "We have left everything to follow you! What then will there be for us?" (Matt. 19:27-30). Jesus' reply directed the attention away from immediate reward and placed it in the context of eternity. "And everyone who has left houses or brothers or sisters or father or mother or children or fields for my sake will receive a hundred times as much and will inherit eternal life" (v. 29). By today's standards, that is a good return on the Dow! Translated to contemporary investment language, for every $100 invested we receive $10,000. Now of course Jesus did not mean to place a monetary value on his answer. And certainly he is not saying eternal life is something we earn, for salvation is the result of grace, not works. But the fact remains: To know that someday we will spend eternity with our Lord and Christian friends is assuring and rewarding.

But there are immediate rewards, too. Just knowing that I am a part of God's kingdom here on earth is fulfilling. There is an old story we have heard many times. Three men were working as construction hands on a building. Each had a different answer to the question a passerby asked: "What are you doing?" One said, "I'm carrying bricks." Another said, "I'm earning $50 a day." The third replied, "I'm building a church!" The privilege to share in the here-and-now experience and to know we are helping to build the kingdom of God is rewarding.

Remember the story of Brother Kulp whom the missionary in Japan thanked for his scholarship grant? Kulp replied to me, "I didn't know an 80-year-old man in a wheelchair could be so useful!" This was as fulfilling to Brother Kulp as building a church was to the third laborer in my story.

Whether we give service to neighbor or friend in the name of Christ, whether we give money to advance the kingdom of God in the name of Christ, or spend time on one or many projects in the name of Christ, each experience is fulfilling and rewarding. Any person who has done it will agree.

The feeling is similar to the experience a faculty member shared with me one day. He was recalling all the students he had in his classes over the years who are now making valuable contributions to the church and community. He said, "And to think that I was paid for teaching!" To be a distributor of the riches of God's grace is truly a reward here and now. And this distribution of God's riches may be conveyed by giving time, by giving service and skills, or by giving money to make it possible for others to give time and skills.

There is yet another variation of the steward's reward in the here and now. This one comes from Hebrews 11. The whole chapter is given to reciting stories of faithful Old Testament persons such as Abel, Enoch, Noah, Abraham, Isaac, Jacob, Sarah, Moses, Rahab, Gideon, Barak, Samson, Jephthah, David, and Samuel. Each of these men and women was tested and tortured (v. 35). Finally, verse 38 says, "The world was not worthy of them." The chapter begins by saying, "Now faith is being sure of what we hope for and certain of what we do not see."

A free translation and combination of verses 4 and 13 might read, "These all died in faith, not having received what was promised, but through their faith story they are still speaking." Here are marvelous examples of "pilgrim people of God" who become the role models for us to follow. Even though they are deceased, they are still speaking through their stories.

We too can be Christian role models (stewards). That is, our influence will continue long after we are gone. Through the giving of time and service a Christian can be part of a great movement within the church. By the giving of money we can assure the continuation of overseas ministries or great works in our own country and community. Consider all these opportunities and more—schools, colleges, orphanages, mission programs, the poor and homeless, immigrants, congregational outreaches, youth work, church camps, retirement homes, hospitals, the handicapped. We can

contribute to all of these causes from our current income or through our wills and estates by giving our
firstfruits and by practicing Jubilee.

We may not be listed on a plaque or be prominent
in historical literature, but we can have the assurance
that we have been faithful and obedient. This is a form
of reward here and now.

The final reward will come some day when we hear
his voice saying, "Well done, good and faithful servant! You have been faithful with a few things; I will
put you in charge of many things. Come and share
your master's happiness!" (Matt. 25:21).

Appendix A

Congregational Long-Range Planning[1]

A Prototype

Introduction

Congregational planning is about people. It's about what they believe, how they feel, how they think and act, and what happens in relationships between members as they engage themselves in continuing the work Christ began. Planning involves your members in their dreams. It invites possibility thinking about what they hope their congregation will become. Planning helps your members to be more intentional, more organized, diagnostic, and strategic in their methods.

Planning enables you to establish a congregational mission statement—the beginning point in planning. A mission statement "sets the sail" of the congregation. It points the direction of your life together and your outreach to others. It is where you focus on your belief and your calling. Your mission statement is an important document!

With a mission statement you will be able to describe the

---

1. This prototype illustrates how a congregation's strategic plan (spoken about in Chapter 8) can become a planning tool for the congregation.

Christian values that will guide the congregation in your caring and helping relationships to others. It can also guide in making lifestyle decisions and in being a helping and caring congregation. These planning steps we call *outcome goals*. Outcome goals describe how you want other people to perceive your members as they interrelate with each other.

Next, you begin to work at a congregational plan which puts into action your congregational mission statement and outcome goals. We call this step the establishing of *program goals*. Program goals outline the methods and procedures needed for your members to be the persons they say they want to be in your mission statement and outcome goals.

Remember, you cannot achieve these great expectations without strong leadership. Planning, teaching, learning, and growing is a collaborative experience between members. Leadership must be directive. That's the role of the pastor and church elders or board.

The congregation's long-range planning prototype below is not complete. There are blanks for you to fill in as you collaborate and plan with your members. The examples given here are to serve as some "for instances" for your members to react to and expand. Examples are given in all three steps of the planning document:

Step One: Congregational Mission Statement
Step Two: Outcome Goals
Step Three: Program Goals

You and your congregational leaders will want to complete and polish the prototype. Make the changes and additions necessary for congregational ownership.

When you are finished, share your plan with your conference officers. This will enable them to walk along beside your congregation as you "live into God's dream."

I. Mission Statement

_____ Church is participating in God's purpose of bringing people into relationship with each other and with God. Our mission is to continue the work Christ began. This involves our members being present in the larger community as a caring, witnessing, reconciling, helping, and inviting congregation. As a community of faith our members strive to help each other be obedient and faithful to the teachings of the Scripture as interpreted by the church.

II. Outcome Goals

(We mean here the goals that mark passage of our members through their years. These outcome goals have to do with acquiring attitudes, abilities, perspectives—a process that will continue throughout life.)

A. To develop a personal faith that is directive, active, and growing.
   1. Members will search for disciplines that foster spiritual growth.
   2.
   3.

B. To empower, encourage, and support members of our church family.
   1. Members are ready to walk along beside fellow members who are hurting.
   2.
   3.

C. To actively participate in our congregation's community, district, and world outreach.
   1. Members are knowledgeable to both planting and nurturing new churches and members.
   2.
   3.
D. To actively work on peace, justice, and poverty concerns.

    1. Members become involved in these local and national issues.

    2.

    3.

E. To encourage those who show potential leadership ability.

    1. Members are able to search out future leaders and affirm them.

    2.

    3.

F. To develop and nourish a personal and family Christian value system that is reflected in lifestyle and other decisions.

    1. Members are able to discern key biblical values that can guide families in their decision making where future direction and destiny are involved.

    2. Family members participate widely in modeling, teaching, and living into the value system agreed upon.

    3.

    4.

G. To have each household participate in the approved congregational and churchwide program budget through both firstfruits and Jubilee giving.

    1. Each member practices firstfruits giving from current income throughout life.

    2. All adult members plan a Jubilee response to church causes at the end of life as they plan distribution of their estates.

    3. All members receive new and ongoing opportunities for giving through the congregation to local, district, and worldwide ministries.

    4. Members participate in an annual open forum where they can discuss and debate the items in the congregation's program and budget.

    5.

H. To actively support churchwide cooperation.
   1.
   2.
   3.

I. Other
   1.
   2.

III. Program Goals to Undergird

A. Bible teaching and theology.
   1.
   2.

B. Youth mentors and role models.
   1. Encourage all youth (junior high through senior high) to accept mutually agreed upon adult mentors to walk beside during this significant period of their life.
   2. Arrange for teaching sessions for mentors on how to mentor effectively.
   3.

C. Values that determine lifestyle and destiny.
   1. Teach the Galatians 5 and 6 list of superior value traits: love, joy, peace, patience, kindness, goodness, faithfulness, gentleness, and self-control.
   2. Control conceit and envy.
   3. Restore sinning members in the spirit of gentleness.
   4. Show caring concern for others.
   5. Relate to people in such a way that our relationships point people to a "destiny."
   6. Help every person to feel influential in some special area.
   7. Provide occasions where family leaders can interact with others in search of solutions when diversity or divisions occur.

D. Money and firstfruits teaching.
   1. Teach that money is an effective tool of service and that we recognize its potential for strengthening the church and for outreach when used effectively.
   2. Plan at least two sermons annually on the biblical teaching of firstfruits.
   3. Through Sunday school class discussions and other appropriate groupings find appropriate ways to confront all members with an annual firstfruits commitment from current income.
   4. Encourage parents to discuss with their children the family's faith commitment and how that commitment is reflected in their firstfruits giving on a weekly basis.

E. Jubilee teaching.
   1. Plan one sermon and several discussion sessions every two years on the contemporary meaning of Jubilee and the importance of demonstrating this belief in one'sestate plan or will. See Chapter 6.
   2. Every five years conduct professional seminars on estate planning and deferred giving. Foundation personnel can direct the seminar.
   3.

F. Courses on family money management.
   1. Review the services offered by your foundation, national stewardship office, or other local qualified persons on Christian money management. Plan annual teaching courses with strong encouragement for young married and single persons to attend.
   2. Give special emphasis on Christian money management in all premarriage counseling sessions.
   3.

G. Church mission interpretation (local, district, national, and worldwide).
   1. Begin with the steps suggested in Chapter 8.
   2.

H. Congregational outreach (local and beyond).
   1.
   2.

I. Affirming and supporting members of the congregation.
   1.
   2.

J. Other.
   1.
   2.

K. Annual Evaluation Plan
   1.
   2.

Summary Statement on Mission and Goals

As you plan, don't hesitate to dream in developing a vision for your congregation. But keep your plan brief and simple! Complexity is stifling and intimidating. Your congregational purpose is to communicate faith and to change people. It is not to build buildings and bigger budgets. However, as people catch the biblical vision of being Christ's spokespersons, your congregation will grow and financial resources will be there as well.

A good book to give further guidance in your planning is that by Kennon L. Callahan, *Twelve Keys to an Effective Church*, Harper & Row, 1983.

Appendix B

How to Plan a Congregational Stewardship Emphasis

Suggestions for Leaders of Congregations[1]

Congregational programs should include occasions for periodically studying the biblical principles and practical applications of Christian stewardship. This appendix offers some suggestions for working on stewardship in weekend emphases, conferences, and workshops.

1. *Assess the stewardship needs of the congregation.* Meet with the church council, board of elders, or other leadership group. Identify the needs and interests of the congregation. Determine the stewardship areas in which members need the most help. (See the checklist below.)

2. *Emphasize the total dimensions of stewardship.* As Christian stewards we are responsible for all we are and all we have—for the gifts of creation and the gifts of redemption. Lead the congregation in considering stewardship in its broadest scope: time, abilities, land, environment, heritage,

---

1. By John H. Rudy. Used by permission.

the gospel, tradition, money, property—all that God credits to our accounts.

3. *Do not neglect the important economic issues.* Even though stewardship is all-encompassing, a weekend conference would be incomplete without examining some of the practical money matters: tithing, proportionate giving, firstfruits, Jubilee, lifestyle, spending, budgeting, borrowing, saving, investing, insurance, wills, estate planning, and retirement planning.

4. *Choose appropriate settings for the conference.* Prime time, of course, is Sunday morning during Sunday school and the worship service. Plan major input and discussions during these periods. Friday or Saturday evening may be a good time for a workshop on personal financial planning. A Saturday morning breakfast meeting may be helpful to businesspersons and farmers. Saturday or Sunday afternoon may be a good time to meet with the leadership group to review stewardship planning and strategy for the coming year. The final meeting, on Sunday evening, could be reserved for input and discussion on the principal issues which surfaced during the conference.

5. *Select topics which address the congregation's needs.* Based on the stewardship needs and interests identified by the leadership group, choose subject titles which help arouse enthusiasm in the congregation.

6. *Schedule input and discussion for all ages.* Youth and young adults may appreciate a workshop on personal financial planning. A session on money matters for women may be appropriate. Older members may have their own special concerns. Businesspersons, professionals, and farmers may have matters to discuss which are unique to their situations.

7. *Invite resource persons who can be most helpful.* The pastor and others in the congregation should be considered. Some district conferences have stewardship secretaries and committees. Stewardship teachers are available from denominational agencies.

8. *Provide opportunities for personal consultation.* Give room to those who consider stewardship and financial matters private and confidential. During the weekend allow time for single persons and couples to meet privately with resource persons.

9. *Give plenty of publicity to the conference.* Put notices in the church bulletins well in advance of the conference. Consider preparing a bulletin insert. Sunday morning announcements from the pulpit will be necessary. Flyers in mail boxes may be helpful. Creative posters on the bulletin board may arouse interest.

10. *Encourage members to make personal commitments.* At the end of the weekend conference it may be appropriate to gently invite your members to make voluntary private commitments concerning their own personal stewardship.

11. *Plan to continue the stewardship emphasis.* A special weekend emphasis or conference may be only the beginning of a yearlong program. The pastor may deliver several sermons on stewardship. Sunday school electives and Sunday evening messages may be helpful. There may be a series of bulletin messages. Additional books on stewardship may be put into the church library with exciting book reports on Sunday morning. Resource persons may be invited back to help expand the special emphasis on stewardship.

12. *Other resources.* Two helpful printed resources are Kauffman, *Managers with God: Continuing the Work Christ Began*, Chapter 8, "Teaching Stewardship in the Congregation"; and Rudy, *Christian Stewardship: Faith in Action*, 184 typewritten pages of resource materials for pastors and leaders.

John H. Rudy
Stewardship Minister
January 1989

Checklist for Identifying Congregational Stewardship Needs[2]

1. ( ) We need to teach biblical principals of Christian stewardship.
2. ( ) We need help with scriptural guidelines regarding financial faithfulness.
3. ( ) We need to increase our giving to conference and churchwide agencies.
4. ( ) We need further teaching on the firstfruits tithe as a minimum standard for proportionate giving.
5. ( ) We need teaching on the biblical concept of Jubilee giving at the end of life (wills and estate planning).
6. ( ) We need help understanding responsible standards of living.
7. ( ) We need to strengthen our voluntary service participation by giving time or abilities at home and/or abroad.
8. ( ) We need help with personal financial planning (spending, budgeting, borrowing, saving, investing, and insurance)
9. ( ) We need help with retirement planning.
10. ( ) We need to strengthen our mutual aid beliefs and practices.
11. ( ) We need to learn how to deal with financial failure and bankruptcy.
12. ( ) We need to learn more about being stewards of the gospel.
13. ( ) We need to train children in stewardship and money management.
14. ( ) We need help in preparing congregational budgets.
15. ( ) We need help in identifying worthy and unworthy beneficiaries for charitable giving.
16. ( ) We need to learn how to assist poor persons.
17. ( ) We need to develop more openness on money matters.

---

2. Adapted from John H. Rudy. Used by permission.

18. ( ) We need to practice better stewardship of land and other natural resources.
19. ( ) We need help with the question of whether to pay taxes which support preparedness for war.
20. ( ) We need teaching on wellness and on physical fitness.
21. ( ) We need further teaching on Christian and family values that guide us in decision making.
22. ( ) We need sermons and discussions on the meaning and influence of money in our lives.
23. ( )
24. ( )

Suggested Topics for Stewardship Conferences

Biblical Principles
    Faithful Stewardship
    Christian Stewardship: In Search of Faithfulness
    Stewards in Practical Obedience
    Christian Stewardship: Belief That Leads to Action
    Christian Stewardship: Pathway to Spiritual Renewal
    The Landlord and the Tenants
    God's Managers
    Toward a Biblical Understanding of Stewardship
    Christian Stewardship and Its Practical Applications
    Christian Values to Guide Us in Family and Personal
      Decisions

Giving
    Firstfruits or Leftovers?
    The Tithe: Teacher of Stewardship
    Jubilee: Step Two of God's Plan to Finance the Church
    Gratitude and Generosity
    New Testament Standards for Giving
    Stewardship Challenges for Living and Giving

Money

Biblical Guidelines for Financial Faithfulness
Money and Following Jesus
The Good News About Money
Faith and Finances
The Dollars and Sense of Christian Stewardship
The Good Life in Today's Economy

Financial Planning

Financial Fitness for Faithful Stewards
Better Money Management for Christian Stewards
Financing Retirement
Christian Money Management in Today's Economy
Effective Money Management for Christian Families
and Single Persons
Investment Perspective for Christians
God's Will Through Yours (Jubilee)
Guidelines for Coping With Money and Economic
Concerns
Christian Families and Personal Bankruptcy

Mennonite Resource Persons for Stewardship Conferences

**Ray and Lillian Bair,
Mennonite Board of
Congregational Ministries**
stewardship principles;
giving; record-keeping
and budgeting
P.O. Box 1245
Elkhart, IN 46515
(219) 294-7536

**John Buckwalter,
Mennonite Foundation**
stewardship principles;
estate planning; giving
12 Greenfield Road
Lancaster, PA 17602
(717) 394-0769

John Friesen, Mennonite Foundation of Canada
stewardship principles and services
134 Plaza Drive
Winnipeg, MB R3T 5K9
(204) 261-0329

Raymond Frey, General Conference Mennonite Church
stewardship principles; giving
722 Main Street
P.O. Box 347
Newton, KS 67114
(316) 283-5100

Paul Goering, Mennonite Foundation
stewardship principles; giving; personal financial planning; estate planning
1110 N. Main Street
P.O. Box 483
Goshen, IN 46526
(800) 348-7468
(219) 533-9511 in Indiana

Lester Janzen and/or Harold Dyck, Steve Pankratz, Mennonite Foundation
stewardship principles; estate planning; giving
125 Main Street
P.O. Box 909
Hesston, KS 67062
(316) 327-4043

Glen Kauffman, Mennonite Foundation
stewardship principles; estate planning
901 Parkwood Drive
Harrisonburg, VA 22801
(703) 434-9727

Daniel Kauffman
stewardship principles; giving; church financing; capital campaigns; meaning of money
1801 Greencroft Blvd.
Apt. 126
Goshen, IN 46526
(219) 533-0270

Stan Kropf
congregational budgeting and churchwide stewardship issues
421 S. 2d Street, Suite 600
Elkhart, IN 46516
(219) 294-7131

Arlin D. Lapp
stewardship principles;
estate planning; giving
569 Yoder Road
P.O. Box 163
Harleysville, PA 19438
(215) 256-1570

Nelson Martin,
Lancaster Mennonite
Conference
stewardship education;
congregational planning;
giving
Oak Lane & Brandt Blvd.
Salunga, PA 17538
(717) 898-6067

Laban Peachey,
Mennonite Mutual Aid
mutual aid principles and
practical applications
1110 N. Main Street
P.O. Box 483
Goshen, IN 46526
(800) 348-7468
(219) 533-9511 in Indiana

Abe Poettcker,
Mennonite Foundation of
Canada
stewardship principles
and services
134 Plaza Drive
Winnipeg, MB R3T 5K9
(204) 261-0329

Ann Raber,
Mennonite Mutual Aid
wellness and physical
fitness
1110 N. Main Street
P.O. Box 483
Goshen, IN 46526
(800) 348-7468
(219) 533-9511 in Indiana

John Rudy,
Mennonite Foundation
stewardship principles;
giving; estate planning;
personal financial
planning; financial and
business problems
12 Greenfield Road
Lancaster, PA 17602
(717) 394-0769

Orval and Dorothy Shank,
Stewardship Ministers for
Virginia Conference
stewardship principles;
congregational planning;
personal and family
finances
R. 1, Box 212
Penn Laird, VA 22846
(703) 289-5363

Merlin L. Stauffer,
  Mennonite Foundation of
  Canada
stewardship principles
and services
76 Skyline Crescent N.E.
Calgary, AB T2K 5X7
(403) 275-6935

Greg Weaver,
  Mennonite Foundation
estate planning; giving
1110 N. Main Street
P.O. Box 483
Goshen, IN 46526
(800) 348-7468
(219) 533-9511 in Indiana

Robert J. Veitch,
  Mennonite Foundation of
  Canada
stewardship principles
and services
50 Kent Ave.
Kitchener, ON N2G 3R1
(519) 745-7821

Robert Yoder,
  Mennonite Board of
  Missions Regional
  Representative
stewardship principles;
giving; agricultural
economics
R. 1
Eureka, IL 61530
(309) 467-2670

My Personal Stewardship Commitments[3]

I want to be a more faithful Christian steward. With God's help I intend to demonstrate my stewardship in the following ways.

1. ( ) I will acknowledge God as the owner and giver of all I am and all I have.
2. ( ) I will find ways to share my Christian faith as a good steward of the gospel.
3. ( ) I will attempt to maintain a modest standard of living which symbolizes and demonstrates my life in Christ.

3. This was designed by John H. Rudy to be distributed to participants after a congregational weekend conference. Permission is granted for use here and for copying by congregations.

4. ( ) I will plan and control my spending by use of a budget or other workable method.

5. ( ) I will exercise caution in my use of credit and will not borrow excessive amounts.

6. ( ) I will save reasonable amounts for future needs and will invest my savings in harmony with my Christian beliefs.

7. ( ) I will adopt the firstfruits tithe as a minimum standard for proportionate giving.

8. ( ) I will make sure my charitable contributions go to worthy causes.

9. ( ) I will help needy persons even if my gift does not qualify for income tax deductions.

10. ( ) I will dedicate a portion of my time and abilities for service in the church, at home and/or abroad.

11. ( ) I will use sound judgment and faith in the purchase of insurance.

12. ( ) I will keep my will up-to-date and will include the church along with family members.

13. ( ) I will try to be a faithful follower of Jesus in the ways I get my money.

14. ( ) I will try to give financial help to my children when they need it most rather than make them wait until I die.

15. ( ) I will seek competent estate planning counsel when the size and complexity of my estate requires analysis.

16. ( ) I will start early in life to save and plan for my retirement needs.

_____   _____

Date   Name

A Stewardship Bibliography

Annotated for Easy Selection

THE FOLLOWING annotated bibliography has been carefully selected to help you with your special stewardship study. Your congregation may want to consider buying these books for the church library. As you place the books in the library, prepare a bulletin insert on the new books. You should note that the authors of many of the books in this bibliography take the traditional approach of limiting stewardship to the management of money. However, Kantonen, Rolston, Thomas, Thompson, and Westerhof support the position of this book. That is, we are stewards of the gospel. Money is one of the tools we use to share the message Christ entrusted to us.

Books marked with an asterisk (*) are out of print. You may be able to obtain a copy from a college, seminary, or public library near you. Most libraries will be able to find you a "library loan" copy.

Applegarth, Margaret. *Twelve Baskets Full.** Harper Brothers, New York, 1957.

A storehouse of stewardship illustrations. The author picked stories with dramatic and spiritual insight related to the giving of money. The stories come from the Bible, contemporary life, and from countries around the world.

Bair, Ray and Lillian. *God's Managers.* Herald Press, Scottdale, Pa., 1981.

A practical and workable financial record book to help individuals and families sort out their daily expenses and organize a budget reflecting their Christian values. The authors say it's "discovering where the money goes." The columns in the record section begin with *Firstfruits* and end 19 columns later with *Overflow*—suggesting that a well-managed Christian home will have some overflow dollars to give as a bonus.

Blue, Ron. *Master Your Money.* Thomas Nelson Publishers, New York, 1986.

A book that places in perspective the management of money from biblical standards. Blue deals with goals, debt, counselling, investments, the miracle of compounding, budgeting, ethics, heritage, and work—all with the goal of being able to share the Christian message. Recommended for persons of all ages, especially the younger and middle-aged married who are establishing life patterns and lifestyles.

Burkholder, J. Lawrence. *Sum and Substance.* Pinchpenny Press, Goshen, Ind., 1986.

A collection of 24 presidential editorials on issues facing the college during the '70s and '80s. The book is recommended as a model for good public relations for denominational boards and agencies, spoken to in Chapter 10.

Fairfield, James. *All That We Are We Give.* Herald Press, Scottdale, Pa., 1977.

This book opens new ways for us to change ourselves and the world we live in. The writer argues that we don't need to surrender to a conformist mold. We can break out together and become what God intends us to be. The 13 lessons can easily function as a Sunday school quarter discussion. The discussion leaders should supplement their preparation by reading Williams and Houck, *Full Value*, which portrays life as a story being lived. The value orientation of Williams and Houck orients the reader to why we do what we do.

Goldberg, Herb, and Robert Lewis. *Money Madness*.* William Morrow & Co., New York, 1978.

This book contains the observations of two secular psychologists about money. They do not describe a good picture! The authors explain the mad and crazy things people do for and with money and the underlying reasons for such behavior. Their aim is to unravel the psychological threads that entangle many of us. Pastors reading this book will make money a priority for their preaching.

Johnson, John Warren. *How You Can Manage Your Money*.* Augsburg Publishing House, Minneapolis, 1981.

Pastors, deacons, and counselors are looking for books they can recommend to persons who want help with their finances. Johnson's is such a book. Here an apparent expert offers guidelines for managing personal finances based on scriptural principles. Do you need to get your finances back under control? Do you want to accumulate additional assets? Do you want to have more money available to manage, give, and invest? These 16 chapters cover many subjects ranging from selecting a place to live to making a will. This book, coupled with Blue's *Master Your Money*, makes a good pair of texts for the personal/family money-management issue.

Kantonen, T. A. *A Theology for Christian Stewardship*.* Fortress Press, Philadelphia, 1956.

An outstanding book on the theology of stewardship.

Kantonen develops the view that we are stewards of the gospel and that we use our gifts from birth (creation)—time, abilities, and money—as tools in our administration of this trust of the gospel.

Kauffman, Daniel and John Rudy. *Congregational Guide Book in Money & Economic Issues.* Mennonite Mutual Aid, Goshen, Ind., 1981.

A special research project with eleven Mennonite congregations during 1980–81 on how to face money and economic issues creatively within the fellowship. The book explains how these churches identified seventeen issues and what steps they used to work at them. See Chapter 9 of this book for a full description of the guidebook.

Kauffman, Milo. *Stewards of God.** Herald Press, Scottdale, Pa., 1979.

The author writes in a warm and popular style. He believes a vibrant teaching program on stewardship and giving will awaken the church and individuals to new spiritual growth.

Kotler, Philip, and Alan Andreason. *Strategic Marketing for Non-Profit Organizations.* 3d edition. Prentice Hall, Inc., Englewood Cliffs, N.J., 1987.

This book should be required reading for board, management, and program planning personnel for any church agency. Kotler adapts current marketing principles to the nonprofit sector. He talks about marketing and public relations being an exchange of want and need satisfaction. The nonprofit agency should search out the hopes and expectations of the supporters and donors. Church agency personnel can adapt and apply these steps to their agency's mission and goals.

Kreider, Carl. *The Christian Entrepreneur.** Herald Press, Scottdale, Pa., 1980.

This book is primarily intended for persons in business. It is an excellent book outlining productive uses of wealth and general ethical principles along with some specific applications. For instance, it treats the Christian's standard of living and includes an interesting section on progressive giving. It closes with a treatment of the unique gifts a businessperson brings to the local congregation. It is written in positive terms.

Lederach, Paul. *A Third Way.* Herald Press, Scottdale, Pa., 1980.

This book sets forth in simple terms some of the key affirmations of the Mennonite faith in contrast to other theological positions. The average person will see the distinctive nature the Mennonite faith takes in light of the commonly held notions about Jesus, the kingdom, the church, and salvation. Unfortunately, the author does not deal with the question of money in this volume.

Longacre, Doris. *Living More with Less.* Herald Press, Scottdale, Pa., 1980.

A pattern for living with less that is not legalistic or threatening. Highly motivational with scores of suggestions that most will find practical. An excellent book for guidance in lifestyle formation or changes.

MacGregor, Malcolm. *Training Your Children to Handle Money.* Bethany Fellowship, Inc., Minneapolis, Minn., 1980.

An extremely practical approach for parents on how to teach their children lasting money-management principles. It is full of illustrations beginning with the younger set, following them through the teenage years. MacGregor recommends parents' matching allowance programs. Scripture quotations are frequently from *The Living Bible*, which sometimes distorts the reading.

Petry, Ronald D. *Partners in Creation.* The Brethren Press, Elgin, Ill., 1980.

Petry writes out of his experience as pastor, as denominational stewardship administrator, and as chairman of the Commission on Stewardship of the National Council of Churches. He appropriately begins by rooting the calling of a responsible steward within the context of faith. He then makes a case for a holistic view of stewardship—a lifestyle of faith that involves every aspect of human existence. Part two of the book suggests a congregational teaching plan.

Piper, Otto. *The Christian Meaning of Money.** Prentice Hall, New York, 1965.

An excellent treatise on money from a Christian perspective. There are easily three to four sermons coming from this book after you digest its contents.

Powell, Luther P. *Money and the Church.** Association Press, New York, 1962.

A splendid history of how money has been used in the church from 100 C.E. to the current time. Powell deals with good and bad uses as well as motives for giving.

Ralston, Holms. *Stewardship in the New Testament.** John Knox Press, Nashville, Tenn., 1946.

A fine classic treatise of stewardship principles based on the teachings of the New Testament writers.

Rudy, John. *Christian Stewardship: Faith in Action.* Mennonite Mutual Aid, Goshen, Ind., 1984.

The author calls this stewardship kit of 184 typewritten pages "a resource packet especially prepared for congregational leaders to help them administer effective programs in Christian stewardship." The Rudy kit supplements Chapter 8 of this book by giving additional tools for teaching.

Stewart, James S. *Thine Is the Kingdom.** Charles Scribners Sons, New York, 1962.

The author is a noted Scottish theologian who shares his vision for the mission of the church in our time. He says the first missionary command to Abraham, "Leave!" is still good theology and is equal to our prayer "Yours is the kingdom."

Thomas, Winburn, Editor. *Stewardship in Mission.** Prentice Hall, Englewood Cliffs, N.J., 1965.

The central theme elaborated by respected theologians affirms that Christian stewardship must result in vigorous missionary activity and that mission must be based on the principles of our stewardship of the gospel.

Thompson, T. K., Editor. *Stewardship in Contemporary Theology.** Association Press, New York, 1960.

A collection of nine excellent papers by as many scholars on stewardship in the Old Testament and in the teachings from Jesus, Paul, the early church, and the 20th century. Four scholars write on contemporary views. The book is the condensed essence of belief from nine stewardship authorities.

Trueblood, Elton. *The Company of the Committed.* Harper and Row, New York, 1980.

Trueblood calls readers to commit themselves to Christ and his kingdom, to enlist in the company of the committed, to claim a vocation of witness in common life, and to care for persons out of Christian love.

Watts, John. *Leave Your House in Order.** Tyndale House Publishers, Wheaton, Ill., 1979.

Planning one's estate is no mystery. It's not difficult. But for many people, it's low on the priority scale. Here is a book written in simple language that covers what most of us need to know and understand before we see our lawyer. It assists in sorting through your own values on how you want your resources distributed at your death. Chapters 7 and 8 give instructions on "How to Teach Your Wife to Be a Widow." The appendix has two sets of forms worth the price of the book: "A Memo to My Wife" and "Information for Your Attorney."

Werning, Waldo J. (1) *Christian Stewards: Confronted and Committed* and (2) *Supply-Side Stewardship: A Call to Biblical Priorities.* Concordia Publishing House, St. Louis, Mo., 1982 and 1986 respectively.

These two books should be required reading for any church leader wanting to begin a congregational stewardship teaching program. Werning has spent over 30 years in stewardship teaching and church administration. He connects biblical theology and human response in a convincing way.

Westerhof, John H., III. *Building God's People in a Materialistic Society.* Harper & Row, New York, 1983.

Another classic on the theology of stewardship, written in the tradition of Kantonen (1956) but updated to theological thought in the 1980s. Westerhof writes from the Episcopal tradition.

Williams, Oliver, and John Houck. *Full Value: Cases in Christian Business Ethics.* Harper & Row, New York, 1978.

This provocative book conveys an idea "whose time has come." It was written originally as a text for discussions in forming Christian values for the businessperson. The authors use the case study approach. The book is much larger in audience than the businessperson. The first 75 pages treat "Life as a Story," and how we, the actors, are following an image or a script that is modeling every action and decision we make. The question most frequently asked is, "What image are we following?" The book is a rare find! It should be required reading for every pastor. This book may bring a new approach to sermon delivery. It is a basic book for making our stewardship of the gospel practical. Discussion groups of entrepreneurs will find the book helpful for eight or nine sessions.

Yoder, Robert A. *Seeking First the Kingdom.* Herald Press, Scottdale, Pa., 1983.

The author is a dedicated Christian and churchman. He is also a family man, farmer, and businessperson. He lives in a community which has certain expectations. The book reflects his own thoughts and struggles on the reality of being a Christian steward as he perceives his mission. Chapter headings like "God's People in the Middle," "The Holy Disturbance," "Ever Since Babel," "Owners or Managers," and "Settled People In Unsettled Times," give an indication of how he faces the issues of life. The book is an excellent discussion-starter for small groups. It can easily be read in one evening.

The Author

DANIEL KAUFFMAN was raised on a farm in Kansas. Early in life he decided to train for the business world and become an executive with Ford or John Deere. The dream was short-lived, but it did guide him to major in economics. He graduated from Goshen College in 1944. After a period in Civilian Public Service, he was appointed business manager of Hesston College, Hesston, Kansas. After ten years of service at Hesston he was granted a sabbatical for study at Columbia University Teacher's College, New York, where he received his M.A. in Educational Administration.

While at Columbia he explored new ways to finance a church college. He was introduced to Henry Endress of the Lutheran Church of America, who gave him new insights about fund-raising as "continuing the work Christ began."

After his sabbatical, Kauffman returned to Hesston College to practice his new learnings. He began a stewardship ministry in the Western conferences resulting in improved finances for all the church agencies in the Western part of his church. In 1961 Kauffman was invited by the Mennonite General Board to be the national director for stewardship for the Mennonite Church. In this position he led the denomination in a churchwide stewardship ministry.

In 1971 he was asked to become the Director of College Relations and Development at Goshen College. He led the college's constituency in an effective ministry of development based on the stewardship idea that we are stewards of the gospel and our opportunity is to continue Christ's work. Kauffman retired from Goshen College in July 1986.

Kauffman married Edith Yoder from Kalona, Iowa, in 1944. Edith was a teacher and homemaker. Together they raised four children, who are now married and have eight children of their own. Edith died of cancer on April 2, 1988.

Kauffman now resides at Greencroft, a retirement village in Goshen, Indiana. Working out of his apartment, he continues a voluntary service ministry in stewardship teaching that is cross-denominational and national in scope. He is a member of the College Mennonite Church in Goshen, Indiana.

Managers with God: Continuing the Work Christ Began reflects many of his congregational and seminary teaching methods.